The Leeds Model Company

1912 - 2012

The First One Hundred Years

An appreciative history

To John,
Best wishes
David Peacock

by

David Peacock

Archivist

The Leeds Stedman Trust

Designed, typeset, and originated by MRM Graphics Ltd, Winslow, Bucks.

Printed and bound in Spain under the supervision of
MRM Graphics Ltd, Winslow, Bucks

CONTENTS

1   Introduction

The publication of this book marks the centenary of The Leeds Model Company, one of the leading model railway manufacturers of the twentieth century, whose products continue to fascinate and delight today's generation of enthusiasts. Founded by Rex Stedman in 1912, the company finally ceased trading in 1967. In 1983 The Leeds Stedman Trust was established to keep the archives of the company, and it is from these archives and with the assistance of many friends and fellow enthusiasts that this record has been put together. Hopefully, it will provide a helpful guide to the range of models and associated products and, with notes on their care, maintenance and restoration, become a means of assuring that the Company, and its founder, Rex Stedman, will be remembered for as long as there are model railways in operation.

Reginald Frederick (Rex) Stedman
1893-1959

David Peacock and Adrian Stedman, Rex's son, first met in 1978. By that time David had a growing collection of LMC models and an interest in discovering more about the company. Adrian held strongly to the belief that his father's company - the third in line after Hornby and Bassett-Lowke - was not receiving the credit deserved for its products, the extent and variety of its product range and its innovative engineering concepts, most of which had come from Rex himself. In due course, and with Adrian's collaboration, David wrote two articles entitled 'In the Stedman Style' published in Model Railway Constructor in 1981 and 1984. Tragically, in 1983, shortly after completing the draft of the second article, Adrian died in a car accident. It was left to David to continue with the mission they had started and, with the agreement of Adrian's widow, Joan, The Leeds Stedman Trust was established.

Currently the Trust keeps a collection of 0 Gauge locomotives, rolling stock and other model railway items representative of the standard catalogue range of the Leeds Model Co/R.F. Stedman & Co. The archive includes catalogues (from 1915 -1967), photographs, drawings, documentation, advertisements, etc. from the early 1900's onwards. David Peacock and his son Marcus are the joint proprietors, trustees and archivists.

The Trust holds a large, but not comprehensive, stock of both original used and unused LMC parts for locomotives, coaches, wagons, signals and track. This stock is augmented by newly manufactured parts using either original LMC patterns or re-engineered tools and dies following the original as closely as possible, but using brass, pewter or white metal (see Glossary) instead of 'Newalloy' and other pressure die cast zinc alloys (see Glossary). Colour photocopies of most coach and wagon lithographs and copies of LMC drawings are available from the Trust archive collection. The Trust also works on and co-ordinates the repair and restoration of models and acts as a clearing house between vendors of LMC products and prospective buyers.

FOR FURTHER INFORMATION

Articles on the L.M.C./ R.F. Stedman & Co. have been published since 1981, and collectively provide a source of information on company history, products and policy.

MODEL RAILWAY CONSTRUCTOR: 'In the Stedman Style', mainly about locomotives, August 1981, and 'In the Stedman Style', mainly about coaches and wagons, May 1984.

GAUGE 'O' GUILD GAZETTE: The series 'Leeds Lines' (copies available on application to The Trust).

'Mansted Foundry', the locos made for G.P. Keen	Summer 1985
'Nettle and Toad', litho stock and motor bogie	Winter 1985
'Wheels within Wheels' LMC wheel and track standards	Summer 1986
'Standard Tanks' Part 1, 1920 series I	Winter 1986
'Standard Tanks' Part 2, 1935 series II	Autumn 1987
'Boxwood to Bakelite' Part 1, coaches 1912 - 1935	Summer 1988
'Boxwood to Bakelite' Part 2, coaches 1936 - 1967	Autumn 1988
'Open Wagons', full history	Winter 1989
'Mass-production 4-4-0 locomotives'	Autumn 1990
'Box vans and Brake vans' Part 1	Autumn 1991
'Box vans and Brake vans' Part 2	Winter 1991
'Methuselah's Donkey, the 0-4-0 tank loco'	Spring 1993

The MRC articles were written jointly by David Peacock and Adrian Stedman. The Gauge 'O' Guild Gazette series, 'Leeds Lines', were written by David Peacock.

More recently, articles on peripheral topics, 'The Hordern Railway' (June 2008 and December 2010) and 'Hargreaves Coal' (Sept. 2009) have been published in The Train Collector, the magazine of the Train Collectors Society.
The Trust has a website with a forum facility, www.leedsstedmantrust.org.

Two programmes concerning the Trust are available on DVD from the Gauge '0' Guild. The first, 'The Leeds Stedman Trust', was originally a Gauge '0' Guild 35mm slide presentation prepared by David Peacock and Jack Ray in 1984 and updated in 1994. The second, 'Augurswell and Great Blessingsby', is a 20 min. video of the Trust layout made by David Peacock and Chris Pettit in 2008. Both programmes show a wide range of LMC products with commentary on their history, etc. The DVD included with this book features both of these programmes plus full colour photographs of models in the archive. Thanks are due to Norman and Pat Childs for their painstaking and time consuming work in taking these photographs and to Chris Pettit for compiling the DVD for the Trust. Photographs which are so indicated are the copyright of Norman Childs Photography and cannot be reproduced without the permission of The Leeds Stedman Trust.

No record such as this book attempts to create would be complete without due acknowledgement of the encouragement and generous support given to David Peacock from the first days of the Trust's foundation. I am particularly indebted to Martin and Jane Bloxsom who have patiently proof read this work. Martin, with his profound knowledge of both the railway industry and model railways, provided invaluable help and guidance. Others, some sadly no longer with us and too numerous to mention here, contributed with advice, historic details, ephemera and models of which the Trust is now custodian. These have been of immeasurable value to David Peacock, whose interest and research into The Leeds Model Company really only began with the acquisition of his first LMC locomotive and stock in 1974. One person above all must be named and that is Adrian Stedman. His unstinting encouragement and profound knowledge of his late father's business form the solid foundation of this work, which is understandably dedicated to him and to his father Rex, the founder of the Leeds Model Company.

Photographs
The photographs used in this book are held in the Leeds Stedman Trust archive. Thanks are due to the following for additional material to include in this book:

Page 30, Wagons, Simon Goodyear.
Page 35, GW Mogul, Peter Zwakhals.
Page 53, Bakelite Wagons, Prof. Cyril Dixon.
Page 57, Wembley Exhibition, Simon Goodyear.
Page 62, LMS Princess, 6200, 'Princess Royal', Paul Cooper.
Page 63, GW 0-6-0PT, Neil Simkins.
Page 63, Hudswell Clarke 2-8-4T, Andrew Gill, The Middleton Railway Trust.
Page 68, Pullman carriage 'Jack the Station Cat', Alan Cliff

2   Rex Stedman

Reginald Frederick Stephen (Rex) Stedman was born in South London on 18th August, 1893. Interested in engineering from an early age, he attended Battersea Polytechnic*, where from the age of 15 he trained as a mechanical engineer. His standard of draughtsmanship was of the highest, as early drawings from this time reveal. Under the heading of 'Eswyn Model Works' he produced scale drawings of locomotives which could be used by model builders. Another of his youthful ventures was 'The Ariel Engineering Works', which manufactured model aeroplanes. In June 1912, Rex became the second person to win the Wakefield Gold Cup (see Glossary) which was open to world-wide competition for model aircraft performance**

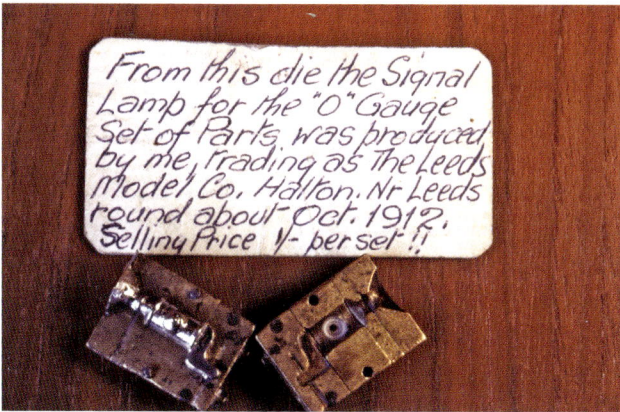

From this die the Signal Lamp for the "O" Gauge Set of Parts was produced by me, trading as The Leeds Model Co. Halton. Nr Leeds round about Oct. 1912. Selling Price 1/- per set !!

Later that same year the Stedman family moved north, to a new home in Wheaton Avenue, Halton, near Leeds. At that address Rex made his start into model railway manufacture and founded The Leeds Model Company. Within a year the business had developed positively with more die cast products being manufactured and the introduction of a model making service. Christmas 1913 saw a small electrically operated Leeds Model Company layout constructed for Messrs Boolds of Devonport (see Exhibitions Chapter 18).

During the 1914-18 war, Rex, although working as a technician in the Experimental Flying Department at the Royal Aircraft Factory at Farnborough, Hants, managed to keep his model-making business going. In 1915 he published his first catalogue (see Appendix A) and established a small number of sales outlets for his products including Bonds O' Euston Road. At Farnborough Rex, who was very interested in photography, designed a wind driven cine camera for aerial reconnaissance. Henry Greenly was also based at the RAE during the war years and he and Rex, through Greenly's magazine 'Models Railways and Locomotives', contributed significantly to keeping the hobby alive during those uncertain times.

* From the early 1900s Battersea was a centre of excellence for engineering students

**The first winner in 1911 was Ernest Twining against whom Rex would later compete in building model locomotives for G.P.Keen.

Soon after the end of the war, Rex moved operations to small premises in Harewood Street, Leeds, and started work on his first 'mass- production' model an essentially freelance North Eastern 4-4-0T. Capital for this development was provided by G.P.Keen. In March 1920 company articles were taken out for The Leeds Model Company Limited, with Keen as Chairman and Stedman as Managing Director.

By 1921, the company had outgrown Harewood Street and moved to much larger premises at Balm Road Mills, employing more people and further widening the range of products, particularly by the addition of litho coaches and wagons all in pre-grouping liveries. Rex married and with a new baby son, Adrian born in 1923, had to make a living from the business. It would seem that this enthusiastic development of the company placed too much strain on Keen's pockets and in 1924 the company was re-financed and restructured by 'association' with the much smaller and technically less competent Bristol Model Company and its acquisitive owner, Hugh Leader.

At this point, Keen backed out of LMC, leaving Rex in his debt and Leader became both Chairman and Managing Director, with Rex relegated to the post of 'Chief Engineer and Designer'. Clearly such demotion did not suit Rex who by nature was a boss, never an underling, and it is clear that he and Leader were often at loggerheads. A further cause of conflict must have been the time Rex gave to reducing his debt to G.P. Keen by making the 'Mansted Foundry' models including the outstandingly powerful LNER Garratt (see Chapter 11).

As soon as he could Rex found a more congenial business partner and financier in R.S. Moore. In 1928, with Moore's backing, and with a move to premises in Jack Lane, he continued the business under his own name, R.F. Stedman & Co. Ltd., 'Leeds Models Continued', with Moore as Chairman and Rex and G.M. Simpson as joint Managing Directors. Simpson had joined the LMC soon after the move to Harewood St., and was Works Manager for several years up to the time of Stedman's takeover of the whole LMC stock, work in progress and order book. However, the times were tough and it is doubtful if the company could sustain both the investment needed for continuous improvement of the product range and pay the wages of management and workforce, large in relation to the company turnover. A serious fire at the works in June 1932 left both Rex and the company with an uncertain future. Two months later Rex withdrew from the business, leaving the company in the hands of Moore and Simpson.

They reverted to the former name of 'The Leeds Model Company Ltd', using as the interim style 'Leeds Models Continued', which Rex had used when he took over the company in 1928.

Away from model railways, Rex returned to his photographic hobby and, with his wife as fellow director, opened 'Stedman's Cinematograph Laboratory'. This was situated almost opposite the LMC factory which had moved from Jack Lane and was occupying a part of Potterdale Mills on Dewsbury Road, Leeds. Here, no doubt with regular trips across the road to keep pace with the model railway business, Rex worked on developing cine cameras and sound-on-disc systems for 9.5mm home movies until the outbreak of the Second World War.

THE . . .

STEDMAN

9.5ᴹ/ₘ

PORTABLE . . . .

TALKIE EQUIPMENT

His interest in aircraft also remained strong, to the point of designing and building in his back garden a full size two seat tandem glider TS-1 called 'City of Leeds'! In his book 'British Gliders and Sailplanes 1922 - 1970', author Norman Ellison details this conventional wooden craft, which had a wingspan of 50 feet (15.24m) and was 25ft (7.62m) long. The glider made its first flight on July 21st 1934 at Baildon, Yorks. It received a Certificate of Airworthiness nine months later and had an active flying life up to the start of the war. This was the only one built, but Ellison was aware that Rex, at the time a keen member of the Bradford & County Gliding Club, had designed several other gliders which were not built and remained as incomplete projects.

From 1939 to 1945 Rex served as Chief Test Pilot at the Blackburn Aircraft Co, flying all types of aircraft repaired at their Sherburn-in-Elmet factory. In 1942, he unwittingly became a member of the Caterpillar Club, the organisation founded by

STEDMAN TS–1. "CITY OF LEEDS"

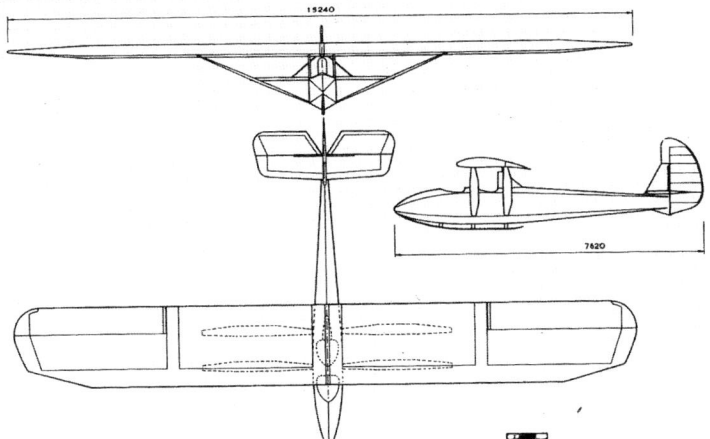

Leslie Irvin in 1922 for any person who bailed out of a disabled aircraft with a parachute. On July 8th, at Dishforth Aerodrome, Rex was pilot-observer in a Hengist glider being piloted by a Flight-Lieutenant French. All was going well during the tow and climb to 11,000 ft, but in a dive the craft began to break up at 7,000 ft. Rex was flung clear and, although hit by some of the wreckage, he landed safely with minor injuries. The pilot, likewise knocked about by pieces of the aircraft, also came down safely.

The Blackburn Aircraft Co. manufactured 1699 of the total 2396 Fairey Swordfish torpedo bombers built. Rex was particularly proud of the role he played in testing these off the production line. He was further delighted when the first Airfix kits of the Swordfish depicted the aircraft which he was flying at the time the photograph had been taken.

The job of a test pilot was of necessity somewhat hazardous, as Rex proved more than once. On a rainy day in October 1945 he landed the Grumman Wildcat he was testing on a slippery grass strip, overshot the end of the runway and ended up nose down in the adjacent field. Fortunately he sustained no injuries in this crash. After the war Rex continued as a test pilot until 1949, working for Chrislea Aircraft Co. Ltd, located at the small Clyst Honiton airfield in Devon – now Exeter Airport. This company produced a low priced, light, all metal four seater passenger aircraft, the 'Super Ace', and from this developed, primarily for the export market, the 'Skyjeep' (selling for £2,250) which was adaptable for cargo or use as an air ambulance. Neither aircraft sold well. Rex left Chrislea in 1949. The company was wound up in 1952.

Almost immediately, in April 1949, Rex, known in the model railway trade as 'Bill Stedman', re-entered the model making business, setting up S & B Productions with the rather flamboyant ex-soldier George Woods 'Ross' Burmingham as his partner. Burmingham stayed less than a year in the shop and works, at 3 Orton Buildings, Portland Road, South Norwood. As with others before him he doubtless found Rex's rather stern and authoritarian temperament too much for a day-to-day business relationship. Just as in his LMC days, Rex very definitely had to be the boss! Undeterred by Burmingham's departure Rex, loyally supported by his wife, Christina Kathleen, his sister Elsie Clucas, a young male manager and two young girls, continued with the business. Together they produced a wide range of items for 00 gauge, a few for TT, and the patented sprung axleboxes for both 00 and 0 gauge wagons and vans. The Dermic precision oiling syringe was another S & B success although it was barred from sale in the USA, as likely to be used for drug taking!

Frank Smith joined Rex Stedman at S & B Productions in 1957, having joined the model railway trade in 1946, working for J.G. Sandford & Co., (Gresham Model Co). With solid experience in model making and the retail end of the business, he set up Crystal Palace Model Railroads in 1950 with partner R.A. Collins. So successful was this business that at one time it was the largest of its kind in the Greater London area. Frank served as manager of the S & B business until Rex, diagnosed with terminal cancer and soon to pass away in Guy's Hospital, left him effectively in charge. Frank would regularly drive Mrs. Stedman to the Hospital and Rex, enthusiastic for the business to the end, would demand a report on progress.

After Rex's death in December 1959 Mrs. Stedman, with the support of Mrs. Clucas, sought to carry on the business. Her son, Adrian, became increasingly concerned for her health and encouraged her to dispose of the company. Ultimately GEM, (George E. Mellor), took over all product manufacturing rights and the unexpired lease on the S & B shop was taken up by Frank Smith, trading under his own name. This retail shop was eventually sold and later became Norwood Junction Models and remains a model shop to this day!

Rex's passing was widely reported in the model press, with due recognition of the most significant innovations and developments he had brought to model engineering. He has left us a rich inheritance of his talents as an engineer and skills as a modeller.

3   MODEST BEGINNINGS (1912–1921)

Shortly after his success in winning the Wakefield Gold Cup, Rex moved with the Stedman family to Wheaton Avenue, Halton, near Leeds. There, in October 1912, Rex founded 'The Leeds Model Company'. His first production items were for signal parts to a finer standard than hitherto available. The set comprised of a gravity die cast arm, bearing bracket, lamp, backshade, lever and counterweight and lever bearing. These are featured in his first preliminary list from May 1915, along with wagon wheels, axleguards and buffers, coach bogies and Mansell wheels and scale 3-link couplings. The list also featured a Great Northern 12 wheel dining car with full interior detail, one of the early hand built models used to advertise the work of 'our junior partner' (none other than Rex himself), who it was stated had 'over twelve years experience of model railway work'.

We are specialists in building small scale rolling stock, and a Dining Saloon we recently built is illustrated below.   This model is complete in all detail, the interior being fitted up in "after dinner" style.   On the tables are books and papers, bottles, SODA SYPHONS with spouts and handles, packs of cards, &c., &c.,   The whole is illuminated by electric light and flexible connections are provided at each end of the coach to connect to an accumulator carried in the guard's van.

Verification of this ambitious specification can be found in a letter from Lieut. E. Melville Wills of Bristol published in the December 1917 issue of Models Railways and Locomotives; *'The car, (made for me by the Leeds Model Co.), is completely fitted up inside with electric lighting; each compartment contains a berth made up with sheets, rugs and pillows, wash basin, towel rail and towel; carpet on the floor, curtain, bell push and communication cord. The attendant's compartment contains cupboards, gas ring and bell and indicator; one smoking compartment has a seat instead of a berth and also ashtrays.'*

The war and Rex's employment at Farnborough would have restricted his modelling activities, but not his dreams and plans. The cover design of a catalogue planned for 1916 (see Appendix A), his move at the end of the war to a small workshop at Harewood Street, and the introduction in 1919 of his first locomotive, a 4-4-0T, demonstrate both his drive and capability. With the exception of the spring, all parts of the locomotive were made at Harewood St. A limited range of coaches, wagons and vans at that time were all hand-made in timber. Inevitably these were relatively expensive to manufacture and Stedman's initial approach to cost reduction on rolling stock and buildings, was embossed card lithography, (Patent No. 164,227). Only one vehicle, a NE open wagon introduced in 1920 was ever produced, clearly also at an unacceptable cost (see Chapter 8). The switch was made in 1921 to flat paper lithographs, also patented, which then continued as the company's standard output until the introduction of moulded Bakelite wagons, vans and coaches in the late 1930s.

Ambitious plans to expand the product range and necessarily employ a larger workforce, needed money for their furtherance and for Rex Stedman the cash came from Geoffrey Keen. Keen was one of the leading influences in the model railway hobby in the last century. For many years he was President, Chairman and Exhibition Manager of the Model Railway Club; the present HQ building of the Club bears his name – Keen House. He was a wealthy man and commissioned many fine models (DVD pictures 78, 105,106), thus supporting several of the model makers and model companies of the time. He also had extensive layouts, K-Lines, in each of the houses where he lived, initially in Kensington, then in Devon and finally in East Kent.

In 1920 Keen provided the finance enabling Rex Stedman to expand the

business and on 11th March the company was incorporated as The Leeds Model Company Limited, with Keen and Stedman as subscribers and directors. The money enabled Stedman to move in 1921 from the small premises in Harewood Street to a new factory at Balm Road Mills, Hunslet, one area of which is shown here. Manufacturing capacity was immediately enlarged, allowing introduction of an 0-4-0 saddle tank, variants of the 4-4-0 standard tank and in addition to the existing hand built wooden rolling stock, production of the first litho coaches and wagons. The company from its modest beginnings was now fully under way.

4   Standard Tank Engines – First Series

The high boiler and bulky outline of the LMC's first series of 0 Gauge standard tank locos was dictated by the need to fit the body around a clockwork mechanism. Introducing the model in 1919 as 'A real victory for a British firm' the advertisements claimed:

'It has often been stated that British Firms were unable to manufacture a Small Gauge Model Loco-motive equal to those supplied by Continental makers at a reasonable price. We set out to prove it could be done, and feel confident we have succeeded, and placed on the market an entirely British-made model, equal in every respect and in many ways superior to those of foreign manufacture'

Stedman's first idea was to have the locomotive top wound through a key-hole in the cab roof. A leaflet published in 1919 describes the mechanism as *'our own design and is entirely different to those of foreign manufacture. It has double springs and the winding is done through the cab roof thus doing away with the unsightly hole in the side'*. The text on the mechanism for the January 1920 catalogue makes no mention of either of these innovative concepts which were not developed. In the event models had a traditional single spring and more simple and direct side winding, this notwithstanding that the loco shown above used to illustrate the 1920 catalogue shows the hole in the cab roof. The first batch of roof pressings with key hole was not scrapped. Instead, the hole was disguised with a 'ventilator' cover. The wheel configuration for the first of the series was 4-4-0 (DVD picture 1) and with minor changes the bodies, produced from a single set of press tools became successively a 4-4-2, 0-4-4, 0-6-2 (DVD pictures 2,3,4) and 4-6-0, shown below.

The 4-6-0 version uniquely had doors fitted to the cab, these serving to conceal the intrusion into the cab space of the rear wheels. These models, introduced before the grouping, were offered in a range of liveries, NER, L&NWR, GCR, MR, L&SWR, GNR, SE&CR, LB&SCR and GER.

The liveries were applied to appropriately coloured bodies as large panel trans-fers complete with coats of arms, lettering and lining. Chimneys, domes and safety valves were varied to suit the 'look' of prototypes of the companies represented by the livery. Models supplied later in post-grouping styles were painted and hand lined with individual transfers used for lettering and number-ing. Similar variations of fittings again completed the impression appropriate to the livery. Driving wheels which were cast iron ran on 5/32" diameter round ended axles and required quartering 'by eye'.

Mechanisms produced from 1930 onwards were fitted with square ended axles and Newalloy zinc die cast wheels (see Chapter 13). All locomotives in the series had 1.1/2", (38.1mm), diameter 16 spoke driving wheels. Bogie wheels, 7/8", (22.2mm) diameter 8 spoke, were cast initially in white metal, later in Newalloy. Coupling rods were nickel plated planished steel. Attention to provid-ing adequate weight for effective traction and hauling power was a key element in Stedman's design approach. The catalogues quoted notional weights for these models (which had no strict prototypes) in the range of 65 – 80 'scale' tons and, allowing 15 tons plus for coal and water, the models weighed between 2¼ and 2¾ pounds, (1.02 and 1.25kg). For specific dimensions and weights of each model see Appendix D.

Stedman foresaw the gradual but inevitable change among enthusiasts from clockwork to electric drive, An 8v DC unit was introduced from late 1924, the mechanism having deep brass frames and assembly complicated by a host of parts including brass frame spacers, brass bushes, brass sleeved Bakelite brush carriers, a high quality cast magnet and different sizes and lengths of screws, some brass, some steel, for every part (see Appendix B). Although rated at the time as one of the best on the market, the mechanism was certainly not cheap to manufacture. Finance of £500 was sought by Stedman and Leader in 1926 for tooling to cut the motor manufacturing and assembly costs. Frank Hornby had offered to purchase 10,000 of the units at 7/6 (35p) each, but without the tooling the lowest price which could be justified was 10/- (50p). The finance was not forthcoming and the deal fell through. This experience pointed Stedman to further developments based on smaller, easier to assemble lower profile electric motors. In mid 1927, Stedman's model of a GC 2-4-2T low boilered tank engine was reviewed in Model Railway News (see Chapter 16). This was the beginning of the end for the older high boiler locos and the deep brass frame mechanisms and the start of the second series of LMC standard tank engines.

5   The 0-4-0 Saddle Tanks

At the same time as the first locomotives in the standard tank range were made, LMC produced a smaller, less expensive, 0-4-0 saddle tank locomotive (DVD picture 5). This model, with refinements along the way, survived into the early 1960s, and was altogether the longest lived model of the entire range! Quite untypically of Stedman, this model ran counter to his approach of producing 'scale' or realistically near prototype models.

Business was most difficult in the years following World War One. Companies we now acknowledge to be the great names in model railways were fighting hard to establish themselves with enthusiastic but none too wealthy buyers. The LMC products were attractive but they were also relatively expensive. Stedman obviously decided that a lower price model was needed to appeal to less well off buyers, if only to act as an introduction to the LMC range, generate an appreciation of the quality of the products and hopefully in better times lead to further sales. However when first introduced in the 1922 catalogue, the 0-4-0 was priced at 45/- (£2.25), only 5/- (25p) less than the standard 4-4-0 tank.

Pricing at this level was probably inevitable considering that in materials and construction the model followed classical Leeds design and manufacturing standards. Made from heavy gauge tinplate and hand soldered, the first locomotives were fitted with cast iron wheels and the standard clockwork mechanism with all parts except the spring made in house. All up, the loco, with power to pull and a long running time, weighed in at just less than 1 kilo – 61 scale tons! Ten choices of pre-grouping company liveries were offered. From 1925 the locos, now with the liveries of the big four, were offered with electric power using the 8 volt brass frame mechanism. The 1¼ inch diameter wheels on the 0-4-0 presented a problem, with the final drive gear likely to foul the central rail current collector strip. The rather inelegant solution, probably copied from other manufacturers, was to place a gear wheel on the rear face of one of the driving wheels and connect this via a small spur gear on the outside of the frame through to the internal drive.

The introduction of a new electric motor, frame design and gear train in the mid-1930s, allowed the drive on the 0-4-0 to be standardised with all the loco-motives then in the range and no further changes to the drive were made throughout the remaining life of the model. Prior to World War II the tank bodies were constructed entirely from sheet metal. After the war, the design of the front end was simplified by the provision of a single piece casting incorporating the smokebox door and the inside cylinder head covers which had hitherto been separate castings. There were two versions of the new casting, one with a centrally positioned number plate, the other with a central hole for a handle and wheel. At some time in the model's life the early 16 gauge (1.6mm) wire handrails were reduced to 20 gauge (.9mm) giving a neater appearance.

In the early 1950s and with the introduction of train sets, (see Chapter 20), the 0-4-0ST was modified with the provision of outside cylinders and since the inside cylinder covers remained on the front casting this model appears to be the only four cylinder saddle tank ever made! The front end of the footplate was cut back flush with the front of the smokebox making the locomotive 5/16" (8mm) shorter than its inside cylinder counterpart, and giving the loco a more squat appearance (DVD 6). At this time smoke generating units were available and fitted into many of the inside and outside cylinder 0-4-0's. Access to the unit was via a sliding cab roof.

From the first the choice of running numbers of the saddle tanks appears to have been haphazard, as well as an ongoing matter of economy. Models were often supplied with single, but rarely with more than two figures. Some of the post 1950 Great Western train set locomotives were despatched numberless!

Over the years many of these long lasting and widely available models have

undergone repainting and changes of livery and number-ing by their owners. The LMC in its normal business up to the end of the 1920s would certainly have supplied any customized livery to order and there is at least one model extant bearing the words 'Leeds Model Company'. A few special adaptations of the model exist including, Mansted Foundry 113, shown here, for Mrs. Keen's Pantry Dockyard railway, and two similarly modified but less detailed models for the Hordern Railway, shipped to Australia in 1928 (see Chapter 11 Mansted Foundry and Chapter 12 The Hordern Layout).

6   Leeds for Bassett-Lowke and others

Collaboration at a personal level between model railway manufacturers was as much a factor in the business in the 1920s as was competition for customers. For the Leeds Model Company, non-branded parts were for sale to all comers and purchases from 'rivals' were equally acceptable if they made up a shortfall, Such cross-trading raises questions today as to parentage, particularly in the case of vehicles fitted with LMC castings, but otherwise not of LMC manufacture. Locomotives are frequently no more readily identifiable, but not in the case of two manufactured by LMC in 1922 for Bassett-Lowke, business facilitated if not initiated by G.P.Keen with his contacts at Bassett-Lowke and financial interest in LMC. Such a helping hand for Stedman and the LMC would have been more than welcome in those frugal early days of the company's development and more than helpful too for Bassett-Lowke. Before the war B-L had sourced many of their locomotives from Carette and Bing in Germany. Carette ceased production in 1915 and Bing stocks were all but exhausted. The persistence of anti-German feelings among B-L customers made further purchases from Bing difficult. Quite suddenly, Bassett-Lowke had become

desperately short of 0 gauge locomotives in their product range.
The locomotives supplied by LMC were a GW Churchward 4-4-0 County, shown above (DVD 7), and a Caledonian Class 72 Pickersgill 4-4-0 (DVD 8). The bodies of these models were of classic Leeds soldered tinplate construction and from the evidence of models surviving today, LMC supplied all but the wheels and mechanisms, electric or clockwork, which were supplied by Bassett-Lowke. Options for County names included 'County of Middlesex', No 3800, 'County of Carlow', No 3801, 'County of Hereford' No 3828 which is depicted in the

Bassett-Lowke catalogue, and the Trust archive model No 3837 'County of Stafford'. The Caledonian locomotive, in blue livery for passenger services, had just the one running number, 77. Reviewing the County in the December 1922 issue of Everyday Science, Henry Greenly commented: 'The colouring of the model follows the latest GWR practice, i.e. green and black without lining. The crosshead and slidebars are exceptionally neat and represent an improvement on the usual model in this gauge'. Greenly was altogether supportive of his wartime colleague's efforts and his editorials regularly covered, often in considerable detail, the latest products and developments of the L.M.C.

Having produced the County and 'Caley' models for Bassett-Lowke, Leeds would not themselves then offer the same locomotives under their own name. It was not in Rex Stedman's nature to allow potential assets to stand idle or go to waste. Using tooling and parts from the County, he produced in 1926 a Great Western 2-6-0 Mogul (DVD 9) and in 1927, using Caley parts and tooling, the Pickersgill 0-6-0 goods locomotive (DVD 10). Even later in the 1950s, and whilst the Mogul itself was still in production it is possible to see the use of Mogul parts – from the original Leeds for Bassett-Lowke County tooling, engineered into the LMC models of Great Western prairie tanks. Waste not, want not, indeed!

Contemporary catalogues of model railway manufacturers and suppliers in addition to Bassett-Lowke reveal how much inter-trading and interdependence existed between the companies. The Milbro catalogue for 1931 features only LMC locos, the LNER 'Director' D11 4-4-0, the G.W Mogul and a Series I 4-4-0 tank, all priced identically to the same models in the LMC catalogue. Having no locomotives of their own, Milbro did not acknowledge them to be LMC models. The LMC models were dropped from the next and future issues of Milbro catalogues, being replaced by their own locomotive range.

Bonds did acknowledge the sources of the locos and other models they sold. Their 1928/9 catalogue advertised the LMC clockwork 0-4-0T and the Pickersgill 0-6-0 goods loco, the G.W. Mogul and a Series I 4-4-0 tank. Their wartime catalogue offered LMC litho coaches and wagons as well as' Metalway' track.

Many of the illustrations of spare parts in the catalogues of both of the above companies are identical to those found in the LMC catalogues of the time. To compete effectively economy in the acquisition and use of materials, manufacturing equipment and tooling was essential. Collaboration altruistically served to support model railway enthusiasts and thus expand the industry, practically it kept costs down and thus improved each company's chance of survival.

7   Great Central and other models

Great Central locomotives ran the occasional through train and headed some of the excursion trains to Leeds. Stedman was clearly attracted to Robinson's engines and selected the G.C.R class 11E 4-4-0 'Director' for his first 'Exact Scale Model' destined for 'mass-production'. His hand built master of the locomotive, 'Charles Stuart Wortley', shown here, turned out with GC style cab and in GC livery, is now part of the LMC collection held by The Industrial Museum at Armley Mills, Leeds.

Despite the renaming of the prototype in 1920 (to 'Prince George') the loco-motive as 'Charles Stuart Wortley' was featured in the 1921 catalogue, which was enlarged and reissued after the move to Balm Road Mills. The recently introduced 0-4-0 saddle tank was on the opposing page. The catalogue for 1923 featured a second exact scale model of the LNWR 'Claughton' which was also offered in gauge 1; and two 'Super- Detail' models, the Urie 4-6-2T of the L&SWR and the new Gresley class A1 Pacific no 1470 'Sir Frederick Banbury'. Both of these locos had been built by Rex Stedman to special order and were also offered at a lower price, to a lower specification of detail and finish. They were also offered in Gauge 1. Typically the Super-Detail Models took between two to three months to build, subject to the buyer's desire for detailing. For the Pacific locomotive Stedman used drawings which he claimed 'were supplied to us by Mr. Gresley specially for the model'. Loco cab and tender were fully fitted out, even to the lockers

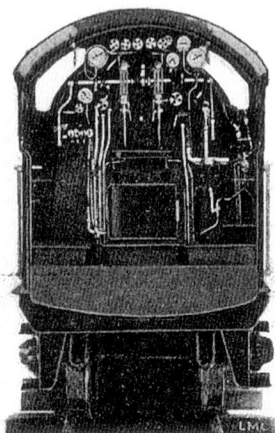

View showing details in the cab of the model "0" gauge "Flying Scotsman."

having hasps and padlocks. The cab itself contained a full set of fittings including all gauges (the water gauges were fitted with microscopic cover glasses), pipes and taps and a special lever which via a Bowden cable could open and close the cylinder drain cocks! A similar locomotive was very favourably reviewed in the March 1926 issue of Model Railway News.

With the exception of the Gresley Pacific, all references and depictions of the super detail models were missing from the Leeds Models Continued 1932 catalogue. The next issue in 1935 carried no mention of any of them whatsoever.

One of the Super-Detail Pacifics was supplied as part of the stud with the Hordern layout shipped to Australia in 1928. One of its shed mates was the only other catalogued Super-Detail locomotive the S.R. Urie 4-6-2T (see Chapter 12). Several examples of the LMC LNER Pacific remain in careful hands today but the Hordern Railway Urie tank is one of only two examples known. Despite continuing searches in collaboration with the Gauge One Society, only one LMC Gauge 1 locomotive has thus far come to light - Claughton 'Sir Gilbert Claughton' No 2222 which unlike the model pictured below was in LMS crimson lake livery.

No additions of locomotives were made to the catalogue in 1924, the year of the Bristol Model Company buy-in, but with money once again available 1925 was marked by a great burst of new models. Stedman's love of the Great Central and Robinson's locomotives was again evident with an updated model of the LNER D10 (ex GC 11E), as LNER D11 'improved Directors' with modified cabs (DVD 11) as well as LNER 4-6-0 class B2 ex GC 'Sir Sam Fay' Class I (DVD 12) and B3 ex GC 9P 'Lord Faringdon' (DVD 13). In addition there was the LNER Class C1 (Ex GN) Ivatt Atlantic 4-4-2 (DVD 14) and, no doubt due to the direct influence of the Bristol Company, two Great Western 4-6-0 Locomotives, a 'Star/Abbey', (DVD 15), and a Castle (DVD 16). Other than the D11, B2 and B3 all of these newly introduced models were also offered in Gauge 1.

The models of the LNER Directors and the B2 were tooled up for mass production. Other models, including for example the B3's which logically used parts common to the Robinson locomotives, were individually assembled and as a consequence small but insignificant variations in dimensions can be found from model to model. Similar variations apply to the other individually assembled models produced in the factory at that time.

In 1927, Stedman recruited H.C. Bradley who stayed with the company in various capacities until 1951. Bradley already had a wide and varied experience of loco building, track making and other aspects of scale model railway construction. He progressed to become chargehand and eventually, in the mid-1930s, after Stedman's departure, was made fully responsible for maintenance and production of the LMC range – by then comprising more than 4000 items! He rejoined the LMC after serving in the RAF during the war, to assist George Simpson with restarting the production of 0 gauge models. Once this was accomplished Bradley moved to sales and from 1947 onwards became widely known as 'The Distribution Manager of the LMC'.* His contribution to innovation and engineering in the Leeds Model Company is nowhere documented, but it is clear that working alongside Stedman, and later with Simpson, his experience, skills and handiwork made an essential contribution to the LMC/Stedman product range.

From time to time models are presented which incorporate Leeds components, or are fitted with LMC mechanisms and which from their build and general appearance could well be Leeds Model Co. products. One such, over which there has been much debate, is an LMS 0-8-0 ex the late Keith Grant**. Another, held in the mid-1980s in the London Toy and Model Museum, is a G&SWR Whitelegg Baltic tank. Clues as to the origin of such models, which carry no maker marks, may sometimes be found by a search of the LMC drawings held in the Trust archive. In the case of the Baltic tank, a drawing (LO/683) was made. No LMC drawing exists for the 0-8-0 but a small drawing of the locomotive from an unidentified supplier was among other non LMC items found in the archive.

Back in 1922 LMC had produced two locomotives for Bassett-Lowke, a GW 'County' 4-4-0 and a Caledonian 4-4-0 with 6-wheeled tender (see Chapter 6). Writing to Model Railway News in April 1927, Leader made it clear that neither of these models would 'unfairly' be sold by the LMC, but the tools and components were used to produce a GW 2-6-0 'Mogul' in 1927 and LMS (ex Caledonian) Pickersgill 0-6-0 in 1928. These two 'new' items both fell into the 'mass produced' category. One other 'Stedman-Super' model, the Ljungström turbo- condensing locomotive, was also featured in that issue, but from then on the locomotive stud progressively diminished until the introduction in 1935 of the second series of standard tanks (see Chapter 16). Post-war productions are detailed later (see Chapter 19).

*Bradley left the company in 1951 to run the Model Engineering Centre in Leeds. In 1956 he was honoured as patron for the year of the Model Engineering Trade Association (META).

** Gauge '0' Guild Gazette Vol. 15 No 4, August 2002 p 21.

8   Rolling Stock

Initially, Leeds Model Company rolling stock was limited to hand-made wooden models. The introduction of paper lithographs not only widened the available range but brought the products, wagons, vans and coaches within the price range of a greater number of model railway enthusiasts. Rolling stock, coaches and goods vehicles were from 1922/3 classified under three headings:

> Type A –'Scale Models'. Wooden bodies with lithographed sides
>
> Type B – Hand-made models of wooden and/or metal construction
>
> Type C – Super detail exact-scale models

Type A – the lithographs

As mentioned in Chapter 3, Stedman's first approach to cost saving in wagon construction was embossed card lithography. In the event this approach did not satisfy his cost objectives and only the one wagon type was ever produced, shown here with LMC working brake gear fitted.

With the benefit of hindsight, we might wonder at the effort put in by Rex Stedman to produce his first coach and wagon lithographs of the old company liveries so soon before the Grouping. He had in fact started preparing the artwork late in 1920 and most of the work was finished and printed by 1921. No effort was spared to recreate as authentically as practicable the principal features, colours, numbering and other aspects of both the coaching and goods stock selected for the initial models. Even today the stunning appearance of well preserved models never fails to excite and impress. A full list of the sixteen pre-grouping vehicles, eight private owner wagons and fifty-three post-grouping coach, wagon and van lithographs appears in Appendix F.

Coaches The pre-grouping companies chosen for the LMC litho coaches were the Midland, North Eastern and the London North Western. (DVD 17–22) In each case the models were a full brake and a lavatory composite coach. The artwork below for the NER full brake shows the outline drawing, the first of many stages of detailing required in preparing the lithographs.

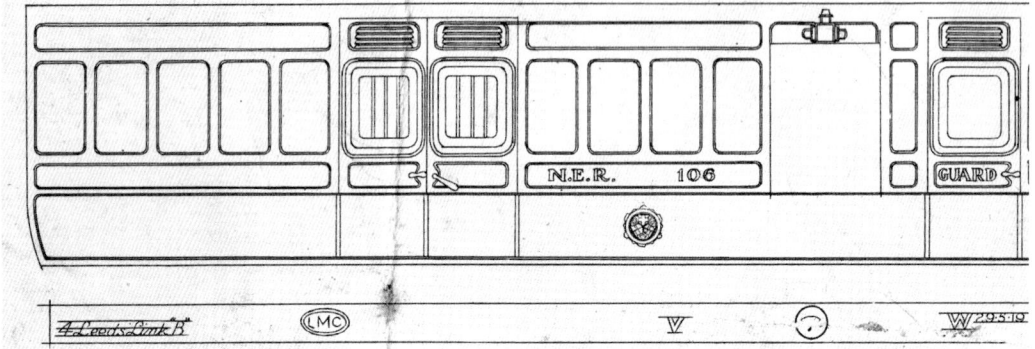

The wooden bodies of this range of coaches were 12" (30.48cm) long, and had end turn-under. The models were fitted with white metal buffers and single link couplings. The bogies were a new design, pressed tinplate, with white metal axleguards (see appendix J). The wheels were white metal with 'L.M.C.' embossed

on the rear face of the flange. Roofs were tinplate. Early models were supplied as shown in the catalogues without roof vents, but these were soon added as an enhancing feature. All coaches were finished with glossy varnish (matt varnish was used on goods stock).

After the grouping Stedman was able to convert the Midland vehicles to LMS by covering Midland and substituting LMS (DVD 23, 24). These adapted coaches were first detailed in the Stedman 1929 catalogue. The ex-Midland coach was pictured together with a new LMS brake 3rd composite coach (DVD 25). The MR/LMS full brakes were listed as available, but only while stock lasted. For the LNWR and NE vehicles no such 'conversion' was available and from 1925 they were described as 'LMS (L&NWR Section)' and 'L&NER (North Eastern Section)' respectively up to the time of their progressive withdrawal and replacement by post-grouping liveries, which was completed by 1930. Regular cut price offers of the older lithographs were made both before and after introducing the new papers. The LNWR full brake, today one of the most difficult of the pre-grouping coaches to find, did not appear in the Stedman 1929 catalogue and its partner coach was offered only while stock lasted.

Lithographs for L.N.E.R. twin and triple articulated teak coach sets were drawn in November 1924 and were introduced in the 1925 catalogue (DVD 26). These were the only short coach lithographs produced, for although LMC later offered G.W. twins and triplets it was fairly explained that these were made by cutting and splicing lithographs destined for the standard 12" long coaches. Articulated sets were not offered after 1932. All of the pre-grouping coaches and the articulated sets had solebar litho strips but none of the big four coaches were so supplied. End turn-under did not feature on the articulated sets, nor on the bodies produced for the new post-grouping liveries. Southern and Great Western were the first of the post-grouping liveries which Stedman tackled late in 1927, (DVD 27–34). Both of these sets of four coaches were destined for a relatively short life, most probably because of loss of the lithos in the 1932 fire. The Great Western 'panelled' coaches with the 'Virtue et Industria' logo were replaced in 1935 by representations of steel bodied stock with the 'button' GWR logo (DVD 35–38). By the end of 1936 the SR coaches were 'Temporarily out of stock' and did not appear in the 1937 catalogue or thereafter, being then replaced in the product range by the much superior Bakelite coaches.

An interesting feature of the SR and GW coaches is that the running number for the coaches - suburban and corridor - is the same, as are the running numbers for the brakes. The reason for this is that each suburban vehicle has one side which is identical to its corridor counterpart, thus only three lithographs are required for two coaches. This economy continued for the GW coaches when the button logo lithographs were introduced, nor were the running numbers changed. The rather plain black end papers for the panelled coaches were carried over for the button logo coaches and are marked LMC 1927. All of the other litho coaches had their own individual numbers.

The two remaining post-grouping coach sets, LMS and LNER, were introduced by Stedman under his own name towards the end of 1929 (DVD 39–46). These were continued until the introduction of Bakelite stock.

After the war the LMS suburban coach side lithographs, coach number 3395, were used briefly as described later for the 'Rigid Litho' coach (see Chapter 19).

Wagons and vans The companies chosen for the first series of six pre-grouping open wagons were NE, GN, GC, L& NWR, MR and GW. As the picture below (from the Trust archive) shows, Rex Stedman photographed actual wagons to use as patterns for the lithography. The NE litho open wagon is indeed numbered V 363, and tare weight, load plate and other details were identically reproduced (DVD 47).

The litho papers fitted exactly to the sides and ends of this series of pre-grouping models, (DVD 48–49) unlike the later post-grouping wagons and vans where the side corner strapping or angle braces wrap around the ends. The first wagons were made from seasoned yellow pine, 5/32" (4mm) thick. Square lock jointing, a concept copied by Rex Stedman from the boxes of Squirrel Confectionery, (his passion was for their jelly babies), was used to connect the sides and ends. Only one pre–grouping box van, in GW pale grey livery, was included in the first series, (DVD 49). This had the same body length as the type B handmade wooden counterparts (4.9/16" – 11.8cm). The post-grouping lithograph box vans were made longer (4.13/16" – 12.2cm).

For the post-grouping litho vehicle range Stedman switched from pine, to 1/8" (3.2mm) thick Latvian plywood. At this point because the space between the thinner solebars was 1/16" (1.6mm) more overall, a 1/16" wider double axleguard was introduced. At the same time Stedman obliterated the 'LMC' letters from the white metal axlebox covers. The lithographs for the post-grouping goods vehicles comprised for each of the big four companies, one open wagon, one box van, and one cattle van (DVD 50–53). In addition the LNER had a bogie brick wagon, (DVD 54), and a bogie high-capacity box van (DVD 55). The LMS had a bogie open wagon (DVD 56), and the GW Siphon G and Monster bogie vans (DVD 57, 58).

Three of the four wheel open wagons were, similar in size to the pre-grouping models, but exceptionally the SR wagon was a high sided eight-plank vehicle and had solebars flush with the sides rather than recessed as with all other stock. (This refinement required an additional thin strip of wood to be fitted between the carrier mounted axleguards and the rear face of the solebar). It was for this complication that the SR wagon was the first to be dropped from the catalogue towards the end of 1936.

Private owner wagons Unquestionably the most popular of the lithograph goods vehicle liveries were the private owner wagons. Stedman launched the first three of these - his own 'R.F. Stedman & Co', green and numbered 36 (his age in 1929), 'J.R. Wood & Co' in its bright orange and 'Brentnall & Cleland', black with white lettering (DVD 59).

As with other lithographs of this time, 'R.F. Stedman & Co. Ltd' was printed in a rectangular plate on the solebar. After 1935, the Stedman wagon was dropped from the range. The rectangular plates on the solebar lithos of Wood & Co and Brentnall & Cleland were changed back to Leeds Model Co. Ltd. These two were joined in 1935 by three further liveries, 'Warrens', and 'Coote and Warren' both

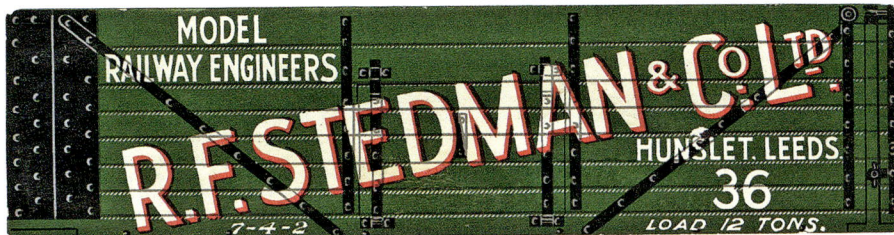

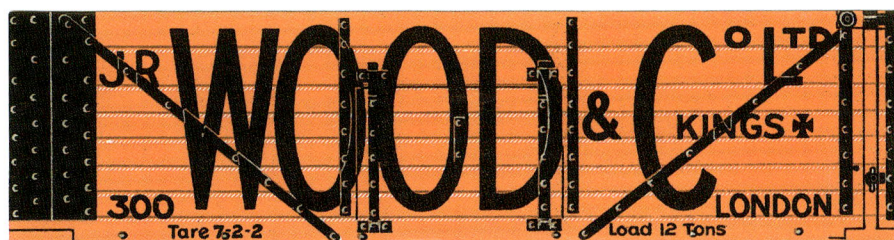

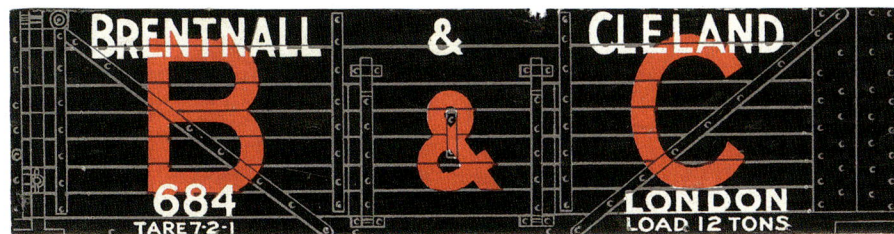

oxide-brown and 'Manchester Collieries' in red. The Leeds Model Co. Ltd solebar plates on these models were oval. Warrens and Coote & Warren differed from the other private owners by not having a drop end. At some stage Warrens was issued fitted with brown painted wooden stanchions fastened over the fixed ends strapping depicted on the lithograph. This gave the wagon a marginally more realistic appearance. Finally, in 1936, two further liveries made the set up to eight. These were 'Cawoods' in black and 'Michael Whitaker' in red. The number on the Whitaker wagon appears to be 100, but in fact reads '100% Service' (DVD 60–62). The Leeds Model Co. Ltd plate on the Cawoods solebar is rectangular.

One more private owner open wagon, never shown in the catalogue, was produced by Stedman in 1927 for the 'Hargreaves Coal Leeds' layout of his friend Dr. Michael Whiting and family (DVD 62). For this special and limited run he adapted the SR lithograph, then the only eight-plank wagon. The first digit of the running number was dropped to change 12340 to 2340. On the solebar the shop out date was changed from '6.27' to '5.27' The 'SR' was of course removed but a perceptible local thickening of the plank line shows the location of the feet of the 'R'. Details on the wagon plate were overwritten. It is believed that some 100 papers were printed, but it is not known how many of these found their way onto wagons on the Whiting layout and how many of these have survived through to today. Several copies have been made and supplied on wagons by the Trust. One attempt to copy the original by Geoff Taylor (Geoff's Wagons, Bardwell Valley), by some 'error' in the scanning or printing resulted in the original black wagon coming out blue!

Brake vans Brake vans for the pre-grouping era were NE, MR and LNWR (DVD 63–65). The LNWR so called 'Palace' van is depicted in the catalogue with full height ends, but an additional paper in the litho set enabled the model to be made up with an open veranda end (DVD 65). In devising the post-grouping brake van lithographs the existing NE papers were retained and joined by new GW, LMS and SR models, (DVD 66–67), each, like the pre-grouping models, differing widely to reflect the prototypes they represented.

'Nettle' and 'Brighton Belle' Two further lithograph sets, bringing the total to eighty one were to be issued before the switch to Bakelite. These were for the Sentinel Cammell rail car, 'Nettle' (DVD 68) and the five car rake for the Brighton Belle Pullman (see also Chapter 15). Neither of these models was replaced in Bakelite. The Pullman coaches were not offered after the war, other than as papers, but the made up Sentinel model continued to be available until the company ceased to trade. Sentinel sets and large quantities of Pullman lithos with a scattering of other papers both pre and post-grouping, were finally sold off in the liquidation sales. The end of LMC was not, however, the end of the lithographs. Several enthusiastic modellers, among them G. P. (Peter) Middleton, Highfield Models, took the LMC papers and applied them to his own bodies made up from much thinner timber than the LMC 1/8" (3mm) ply. This gave open wagons in particular an altogether more realistic appearance, and a good number of these models are still around today*

Type B – The hand built stock

The type B goods vehicle range available in both 0 and 1 gauge at its fullest extent comprised no less than eighteen models (see list). Many of these still survive in good running condition, a credit both to the materials used and the soundness of construction. These models were con-structed from yellow pine and fitted with standard LMC cast parts. All metal construction (with the exception of the bol-sters) was however used for the 30 ton bogie timber truck. The Tar wagon tank was a soldered up metal box, this giving a far neater appearance than the solid wooden blocks used by other companies.

The Type B model range DVD xx and appendix G for models not in the archive

Open wagons and box vans 69, 70
Four and six wheel brake vans 64, 66, Page 91
High capacity bogie vans and wagons 71, 72
Paired single bolster timber wagons 74
Stores Dept. drop side wagons Page 92
30 ton bogie timber trucks 75
Standard cattle wagons 70
Oil and tar wagons 76
Ballast wagons Page 92
GW shunters truck 69
GW Siphon G and Siphon H 73
NE and GW Horse boxes Page 93
LNER tube wagon Page 92

The listing here is taken from the catalogue of 1926/7, the final LMC issue before the R.F. Stedman & Co. catalogue of 1929. In this the type B stock, with the exception of the oil tanker, do not appear, and are not subsequently seen again. The oil wagon itself features in the 1932 Leeds Models Continued catalogue but was dropped for the next, 1935, issue. The oil tanker is of particular interest because initially the tank was turned up from wood. Strapping and other items were attached and the livery and owner name were applied by hand painting. 'Royal Daylight' was the livery depicted in the 1922/3 catalogue, but the only example of the model seen to date is 'Mex Fuel Oil' pictured over.

* Middleton also made up locomotives, the 0-4-0ST and the LMS Ex L&Y 2-4-2T from parts similarly purchased in the liquidation sales. Prior to this involvement with 0 Gauge models, Middleton's speciality had been N gauge. We have the LMC in liquidation to thank for bringing him into 0 Gauge with the benefit and variety of his subsequent Highfield Models products.

At some time between 1925 and 1926/7 the method of manufacture of the tanker was changed. The wooden cylinder was replaced by a tank rolled up from tinplate with square fitted soldered ends and the livery, depictions of rivets, strapping and other details were applied by a large single varnish-fix transfer, BP Motor Spirit, as shown below right.

Type C – Super detail exact scale models

Type C models used to illustrate the early catalogues were destined for G.P. Keen's 'K- Lines' layout. Outside of K-Lines stock there would appear to be few survivors as compared to the Type B range. There would in any event have been far fewer of these substantially more expensive models made. Type C models suffered a similar fate to those of Type B and were not listed in the catalogues after 1932.

The wagon above, for K-Lines, photographed in 2010 is exactly the one used to illustrate the Type C models in the 1925 catalogue.

9   Special Projects

Although the Leeds Model Company was primarily a supplier of model railways, Rex Stedman did not limit himself to railway modelling, nor to the advertised range of the company. Like many other model engineers at the time, if the price was right, he would make it – whatever it proved to be! Thus we find him during his time at Farnborough producing items contemporary with the period of hostilities, such as wooden models of lorries, ambulances, 0 gauge ambulance coaches and a diecast model of the French 75mm Howitzer. In 1918 he produced a model of the battleship 'Kultur', which was used in the Royal Aircraft Factory Peace Carnival. There were also various models of the Scherzer roller lifting bridges to provide access into railway rooms and plate girder bridges.

Building coaches, goods stock and locomotives to the frequently demanding designs of G.P.Keen took up many hours of Stedman's 'free' time. In his 'Model Railway Notes' book, he identifies twelve K-Lines coaches built between October 1917 and March 1919. Day after day his impeccable handwriting records the time spent usually in the evenings from 8.30 or 9.00 pm into the small hours, as well as weekend afternoons and evenings. Keen's observation saloon which was exhibited at the 1925 Model Railway Exhibition accounted in all for over two hundred and twenty hours of painstaking work, complicated by revisions and added details as the work progressed.

In his notebook Stedman comments that work on the observation saloon was halted in order to build a 'Super-detail' model of the N.E.R. Raven Pacific 'City of Ripon'. This was a hurried, but never compromised project. The model was drawn at home on April 20th 1925 and work commenced at Balm Road Mills on April 26th (Sunday!). Three hundred intensive hours later on June 28th the model, shown below, was finished.

In his catalogues of the time Stedman boasted 'When better models are built, LMC will build them'. Today, when City of Ripon(kept carefully in private hands) is on display, it somewhat shows its age. However, it remains a superb example of Stedman's model-making skill and dedication to detail. Rex's concentration on the practicalities of representing the prototype effectively in small scale is exemplified on the model which has a fully removable back head, perfect in detail, yet impossible to have been put together in situ, or fully appreciated thereafter.

Reported in the February 1928 issue of MRN, but featured once only in Stedman's 1929 catalogue, and shown below, the Super-Detail model of the Ljungström turbo-condensing locomotive was, by report, built by J.S. Beeson, (Allen Levy, 'A Century of Model Trains').

Stedman and Beeson, both at the time making models for G.P. Keen, would certainly have known one another. Pictures of Beeson's early locomotives for Keen appear in Stedman's photographic archive. Beeson might well have been used by Stedman to build some of the Super-Detail models at times when the LMC work load exceeded even his seemingly inexhaustible capacity for model making. In his book on Beeson, Richard Ganderton suggests that even the LNER Garratt (MF 110 – see Chapter 11) was built by Beeson, but this is absolutely not so. It is believed, however, that Beeson may have collaborated with LMC after the war and produced to a higher than normal standard a few of the outworked models offered at that time (see chapter 19).

Two models of Gresley's LNER K3 were produced between 1926 and 1927,

but neither was ever pictured in any catalogue. One, shown over, was built for Frederick Rush, a private customer in England and is now in keeping with the Trust (DVD 77). The other, one of the Hordern railway stud named 'Wooloomooloo', is known to the Trust and is in private ownership in Australia (see Chapter 12).

Despite the growth in sales of 'scale model' litho coaches, the company continued to supply small numbers of 'best quality and super detail' true scale models of coaches. Two such models illustrate the 1926/7 catalogue. The lower illustration, a twelve wheel E.C.J.S. sleeping car, had been used in catalogues from 1922 onwards. The LMS saloon coach depicted at the head of the page was one of a rake. Three of these coaches in original condition were advertised and sold on eBay in February 2009. In their 1920s catalogues LMC regularly claimed that 'the variety of coaches we have made is so large that practically every pre-grouped Railway Company's stock has been reproduced at some time or another'. This may well have been true, but it is most likely that these were single orders; for example no other coaches even remotely similar to those LMS items above have been observed in all the time the Trust has been active.

Superior even to the Super–Detail models (called Stedman-Super Models under the R.F. Stedman & Co. regime) were the 'Exhibition Model' locomotives built by Rex Stedman. The Science Museum is home to one of a few of such specials - the Kitson Meyer 2-8-0-8-0 articulated locomotive of the Great Southern Railway of Spain. This model built in 1922 is, like his other 'glass–case'

models, complete with every detail found on the prototype. The models were to 7mm to 1ft (0 gauge), but had exact scale tyres and flanges on the wheels and were set on what we would now call 'Scale Seven' track. Another fine model used to illustrate his 1929 catalogue was a narrow gauge 'Pacific' loco of the Federated Malay States Railways. The whereabouts of this model is not known.

In addition to the specials all standard locomotives were offered with special finishes, personalised liveries and names to suit the customer's fancy. The Lord Mayor of Leeds, John Arnott, was presented with a model of 'the Great Central 'Director' 4-4-0 in 1925 at the Grand Pygmalion, Leeds, when he opened the display of the LMC 'Wembley' model railway layout (see Chapter 18). The loco, finished in LNER livery carried Arnott's name and the number 1925. The cab and tender of the model were fully fitted with backhead and firing tools.

The LMC catalogues up to the time when Rex Stedman operated the company under his own name, offered many of the products in both gauge 0 and gauge 1.

However, and clearly from evidence, the company was quite willing to supply models in larger gauges; witness a superb rake of five Gauge 3 LNER teak coaches, of which the above, recently photographed, is one example.

In the year following, at what was by then R.F. Stedman & Co; the staff built two scale length International 'Golden Arrow' Pullman cars for 'exhibition purposes'. The drawing of the crest is shown here. One of these crests held in the Trust archive shows it to be a masterpiece of engraved brass work. In addition to the crests, the coaches were fitted with all main external details including brake gear, gas and water cylinders, screw couplings, safety chains, brake and steam heating pipes and full roof equipment. Unlike earlier special models (for example those for G. P. Keen) these coaches had no interior fittings. If they have survived, their whereabouts is unknown.

10   R.F. Stedman & Co. Ltd

Rex Stedman was clearly both hard working and very ambitious. Never short of new ideas, he was also given to ensuring that the standard of existing products was strictly maintained. Frederick Rush, who had known Stedman from 1921, claimed 'He was a near genius and suffered the faults of one so talented'. LMC was Stedman's company and he was the boss. He certainly acted like the boss, despite his demotion after acquisition of the LMC by Hugh Leader, the Bristol Model Company Managing Director. Inevitably the conflict between Stedman and Leader became unbearable and Stedman left the company. Behind the scenes he had been looking for a more amenable business partner for some time. A major deterrent to any prospective lender or investor was the debenture in the LMC, held by Leader's brother, which in the event of liquidation would have preference over a loan or ordinary shareholding.

Rush was approached by Stedman to buy LMC out of the clutches of the Leaders. Rush's opinion was that about £5,000 would be required. He himself had about £3,000 and asked Stedman and Simpson each to provide £500, the balance of £1,000 coming from a relative of Rush's who would guarantee an overdraft to that amount. On this basis a private limited company could be formed. Neither Stedman nor Simpson could come up with the cash and the potential deal fell through. A letter in the archives from R.S. Moore to Stedman, dated December 1927, enclosed a cheque for £50 and offers a loan of a further £50 for early 1928. It is not clear, in light of Rush's analysis, how such small sums could contribute significantly to Stedman's purchase of the LMC, essentially lock, stock and barrel. Clearly more substantial sums were obtained in the interim, and in September 1928 purchase the Company he did. From new premises in Jack Lane Stedman set about updating the product range, particularly the litho coach and wagon stock. Here his new company nameplate, his own, is proudly affixed to the smokebox of a GW Mogul.

Aiming for economy and cost saving he dropped the Type B hand built wagons, but did not hold back on special models, particularly locomotives which to the right buyers represented significant income to the company. It was essential in obtaining the highest prices that there should be no compromise in detail and quality. The following description of a gauge 0 'Royal Scot', written in Stedman's own hand and dated March 1928, is held in the archive:

'Body work constructed of best quality materials, all parts hand fitted and all joints soldered. Boiler bands and beading as on original. Side and front windows of cab glazed with "Celastoid". Firebox back of correct shape and made detachable (as City of Ripon Chapter 9). All boiler mountings as on original, including the "Dreadnought" ejector and large ejector valve on the L.H. side. Sand boxes and pipes to wheels. Dummy Silvertown mechanical lubricators. Sprung non-locking buffers. Screw couplings. Flexible brake pipe connections. Nameplate in engraved brass. Number on front of smokebox to be an engraved plate. All steps and handrails as on original. Dummy brake gear on driving and coupled wheels. Cylinders of correct design and finish. Full Walschaerts valve gear, all rods fluted. Radius rods not to reverse in links. Coupling rods with correct design ends. Vacuum pump fitted to guide bar on L.H. side to work from crosshead. Motor: Special design having powerful permanent magnet. 8 pole drum armature wound in eight sections for 12 volts. Commutator and brush gear of special design and construction. Crown and compound gearing of approx 20 to 1.Stop start and reverse switch fitted. Third rail spring collectors on engine and tender. All wheels of turned cast iron. Tender of correct design, beaded as on original. Fitted with tank divisions, seal plates, top cross bar with racks, with shovel etc. supplied. Fillers and pick up dome, brake handles etc. Finished in correct L.M.S. colour and lining. Name as selected. Price £40.00. For two locos ordered at the same time £70.00.

The principal achievement of the 'new' company was completion of the updating of the litho range of coaches and goods vehicles. The letter accompanying the eight page leaflet detailing the new stock boasted, 'A striking feature of our first year's work is apparent when examining the prices of this new rolling stock. Not only have we put on the market the largest number of vehicles in one season, but the reduced prices must prove to you that our policy is to offer scale models at such low figures that they compare favourably with cheap toy productions which have no pretence to scale and detail'.

On his personal letterhead at the time Rex described himself a Consulting and Constructional Model Engineer. His catalogue includes a model of an economiser (see Glossary) and the Trust archive includes a picture of another. He may well also have dabbled with 12" to the foot manufacturing and produced a small car, shown here. The 'Stedman' badge on the radiator may well apply to the whole vehicle – we shall probably never know!

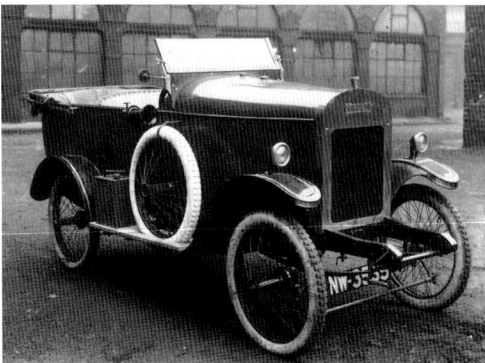

11   Mansted Foundry

'Mansted Foundry', a play on Rex Stedman's surname, first appeared in 1926. By that time Hugh Leader of the Bristol Model Company had firmly established himself in both the Chairman and the Managing Director's seats at the LMC Balm Road works. Rex Stedman was not only suffering from his demotion to 'Chief Engineer and Designer', but also from the burden of debt owed to Keen for supporting the Leeds Model Company up to the point of the Bristol intervention. Throughout his association with Keen, whom he usually addressed as 'Chief', Rex had built a number of fine items of rolling stock to Keen's exacting and critical standards, for the K Lines layout. Rex's workbook dating from 1917 lists work of many hundreds of hours, often into the early hours of the morning, on a range of finely detailed coaches (seven of which are held by the Trust).

As the K-Lines layout expanded and more locomotives were needed, Mansted Foundry was 'set up' as one of the companies able to fill the bill. Using standard LMC parts wherever he could, Stedman set about detail design and build of a range of unique and mainly freelance locomotives for his demanding former patron. These were specials in every way: the bodies were of brass, not the usual LMC tinplate, and the high power mechanisms, 20v dc, had cobalt steel magnets and eight pole armatures. Current collection was from an outside third rail. The locomotives were well detailed and carried on their black bodies the twin transfers of K lines and a small rectangular brass plate inscribed 'Mansted Foundry' with the model's serial number.

Working under pressure, as he invariably was, Stedman did not do all of the design work nor all of the building of every locomotive in the series.

The Model Railway News April 1927 carried the following notice:

New 2-6-0 Locos for the "K" Lines

To meet the growing traffic on the "K" Lines, the elaborate gauge O railway Mr. Keen is installing, four new 2-6-0 type locomotives have recently been delivered. These have been constructed by Mansted Foundry to the design of the Chief Consulting Engineer, Mr J.C. Cosgrave. Owing to the pressure of work at the foundry, subcontracts were placed with Messrs. Winteringhams Ltd. for the boilers and frames and also for the motors; the remainder of the work being completed at the foundry.

There are two classes of locomotive Nos. 321 and 322 (MF 101 & 102) having 5'6" diameter wheels and Nos. 331 and 332 (MF 103 & 104) 6ft 8inch diameter. The first of these is primarily intended to work fast fish, meat, and perishable traffic, while the larger wheeled engines will be employed on moderately heavy passenger trains, chiefly excursions.

In the 'Mansted Foundry' series, the outstanding piece-de-resistance is the LNER Garratt, no 2492, (MF109) now held in the National Railway Museum, York. Dozens of drawings and sketches held in the Trust archive attest to the obsessive attention to detail which Rex gave to this model. In this he was no doubt goaded by the knowl-

edge that Keen had also ordered a similar loco from Ernest Twining. In the event the better model, Stedman's, was kept by Keen, Twining's model was passed to Keen's close friend William Kelly for operation on his Gutland Railway, (See Glossary). Following Kelly's death, it went as an item of the GUR-RUG* layout to Southern France and the Museum of the Wheel (Museon de Rodo) owned by Henry Girod D'Eymery at Uzes. The locomotive is currently held at the Musee du Train, Arpaillargues near Uzes.

Reputedly and untypically, while building the Garratt, Rex was locked for hours in his room at the works. Photographs and drawings in the Trust archive detail the painstaking progress towards completion when, as the front cover of this book shows, the loco hauled Rex, Keen and friend Sir Francis Layland-Barratt - 39 stones (247 kilos) in all - on a short test track. When finished, the loco would haul 104 trucks on the K Lines tracks.

*GUR-RUG = Gutland Uzes Railway – Reseau Uzes di Gutlande

Not all of the Mansted Foundry series of locomotives were destined to work the K Lines. Of the 19 models bearing the plate, eleven went to Keen, one more to his wife's Pantry Dockyard Railway. A further five went to Australia with plates marked 'Leeds Model Co Ltd MF xxx' as part of the Hordern Layout, and two were kept by Rex, either not being taken up by Keen or any other potential buyer, or simply for his own use.

Details and known locations of the Mansted Foundry Models are listed here:

MF No	Wheel Arrangement	Description	Location
101	2-6-0	K lines 321	Not known
102	2-6-0	K lines 322	Musee du Train, Uzes
103	2-6-0	K lines 331	Private collection in UK with MF116
104	2-6-0	K lines 332	Not known
105	2-6-0	K lines 326	Not known
106	2-6-0	K lines 336	LST archive DVD 78
107	4-6-0	K lines 311 rebuilt 'Prince of Wales'	Not known
108	-	Traction engine on truck	Private collection in UK
109	2-8-0-0-8-2	2492 LNER Garratt	NRM York
110	4-6-2	Hordern LNER A1 Pacific 'Sydney'	Private collection in Australia – repainted in LNER livery
111	2-6-0	Hordern LNER K3 Mogul 'Woolloomooloo'	Private collection in Australia – converted to LNER no 1935
112	4-6-2T	Hordern Urie SR H16 'Redfern'	Australia with Hordern Layout
113	0-4-0T	Possibly 'Milton' or 115 is Milton	Australia with Hordern Layout or not known*
114	0-4-0T	Pantry Dockyard Railway	Not known
115	0-4-0T	Possibly 'Milton' or 113 is Milton	Australia with Hordern Layout or not known*
116	4-6-0	K lines 313	Private collection in UK
117	4-6-0	K lines 312 rebuilt 'Prince of Wales'	Private collection in UK
118	4-4-0	LST rebuilt as LNER 5507 'R.F. Stedman'	LST Archive DVD 79
119	4-4-0	LST restored as LNER 5500	Leeds Industrial Museum

The Hordern Layout

In 1928 Rex Stedman received an order for a complete working model railway from a branch of the wealthy Hordern family in New South Wales, Australia. Every effort was put into making this as subsequently described 'a very complete model railway system'. The layout was shaped to fit into a designated room in the family home and measured 17ft (5.2m) x 9ft 3", (2.8m). It has a five road terminal station with an imposing hotel building, a through station, three engine sheds, goods and coal offices, a turntable and a coaling stage, two small and one large main signal box which housed a 60 lever frame.

Rex Stedman at the controls of the layout. Test running prior to shipment to Australia

The layout consisted of a double main line with a complicated array of points and crossings leading to the terminus, engine road and main shed. There was a four road goods siding, 'Darling Harbour', with a shunting neck. The signals were electrically operated with working lamps, the wires to these being elegantly recessed into grooves in the signal posts. Points on the main line were mechanically operated via levers and rodding from the main signal box; points in the goods yard was operated by throw over hand levers. Points and signals were fully interlocked. Small switches and push buttons controlled non-signalled roads and dead ends. Track was laid for outside third current collection, 12v DC. The conductor rail used was the recently introduced brass trapeziform section soldered directly to the heads of countersunk brass screws.

Three LMC 'Super Detail' locos and two modified 0-4-0 saddle tank engines (see Chapter 11) went with the layout. Rakes of main line bogie coaches and articulated sets were painted in a special orange livery with black roofs. There were 36 items of goods stock. Those designated to run at the ends of rakes were fitted with the LMC automatic coupling (see Appendix H). The layout was duly delivered, but sadly was not appreciated by its intended owner and after being put aside the railway and much of the stock was lost. In fact the layout had been purchased in the 1950s by an electrician who subsequently moved up to Queensland. He took the layout, but only two locomotives, probably all of the coaching stock and less than a third of the original 36 goods vehicles went with it. The layout was discovered by Bruce Macdonald in Queensland in 1985, stored rather carelessly under the owner's house. It was in very poor condition indeed.

After two changes of ownership its restoration is now well in hand, as shown over. Supports for the baseboards have been constructed from new. Only one of the solid wooden baseboards was warped and required replacement. Fortunately this was a section of double track without points or crossovers. The buildings have likewise been renovated and, using photographs of the layout as a guide, lost buildings and other features have been reconstructed to resemble the original as closely as possible. Replicas of the original simple wooden buffers were made for the goods yard sidings and the elaborate soldered tinplate strip supports for the glass roofs of the station were recreated using a damaged original support as pattern.

One rake of coaches in the original Hordern orange livery came back to England in the 1970's, was purchased by the Leeds Stedman Trust and returned to Australia to join other rolling stock on the layout. These model coaches must hold the world record for travelling, 37,000 miles in all, quite apart from any distance run on the layout!

The two locomotives recovered with the layout were Gresley A1 Pacific (originally unlined black and named 'Sydney' now restored and repainted in LNER green livery as No. 4470 – see over) and Urie H16 4-6-2T 'Redfern' (now repainted in Southern Railway livery).

The plates on the smokeboxes of these locomotives differed from those used for G.P. Keen's Mansted Foundry models in that they read 'Leeds Model Co. Ltd. MF xxx. Both locos have long been in good hands as have most of the coaches, although several of these have been repainted in GWR chocolate and cream.

Much later, in 2009, the Gresley K3, 'Woolloomooloo' and one of the 0-4-0 tanks named 'Milton'* were recovered with more of the goods stock. Both locomotives were in very poor condition, with mechanical damage, missing parts and heavy rusting. The goods stock was equally battered. In the worst case only the roof and floor with axleguards in place remained of a six wheel brake van. Both locos and much of the stock have now been restored and have joined the balance of the collection held with the layout. As work continues in Australia with the reconstruction of the railway the aim remains to have the layout operational with as many as possible of the original locomotives and items of coaching and goods stock by 2012, to mark the centenary of the Leeds Model Company.

The author at the controls of the layout as restoration progresses – Tasmania 2007

*Milton when recovered carried no MF plate, it cannot thus be determined whether Milton is MF 113 or 115

13   Newalloy

The first models produced by the LMC used cast iron for locomotive wheels and white metal for coach and wagon wheels. Looking for cost reduction and quality improvements Stedman started to explore the pressure die casting of zinc alloys. In 1927 he paid a visit to the Bing factory in Nuremberg and saw at first hand the production of precision finished parts by injection moulding. He ordered a large batch of spoked wagon wheels (marked 'REMOD on the rear face of the flange) and used these from 1928 until his own casting plant, manufactured within the LMC works, was set up in the Jack Lane factory in 1929. From then on Mansell coach wheels, and spoked and four hole disc wagon wheels were supplied in what Stedman called 'NEWALLOY'*. Dies for loco driving and bogie wheels, particularly those destined for the second series of standard tanks, followed more slowly. The full range of Newalloy wheels was offered for sale separately from early 1933 and were fitted to all locomotives thereafter**.

To avoid further controversy after the severe criticism of his first designs (see Appendix C) Stedman adhered to 'steamroller' sizes for white metal wheels. Designing with Newalloy he reduced the tyre width for rolling stock from 5.5 to 4.0mm and the flange depth from 2.5mm to 2.0mm. Similar reductions to tyre width applied when Newalloy was used to replace cast iron for loco and tender wheels, but the flange depth was further reduced to 1.5mm, making these wheels at the time among the most realistic in appearance available.

In the January 1931 issue of Model Railway News, the Company advertisement claimed that *'during the past year we have sold over 200,000 'NEWALLOY' wheels for rolling stock'*. This is an incredible figure for the time, representing perhaps 30,000 to 40,000 vehicles, and not that many were sold by LMC themselves! If true, then substantial customer retrofits and inter trade must have made up the greater part of this remarkable number. The same advert also addressed the issue of the alloy colour which had led some modellers to suggest that the company had reverted to using white metal. The riposte was emphatic! *'We wish to make it clear throughout the Model Railway World that "NEWALLOY" wheels are NOT ORDINARY "WHITE METAL" CASTINGS but an aluminium (sic) base alloy that has been proved and tested by exhaustive trials, and found equal to cast iron in many respects and far superior in others.*

*Adrian Stedman affirmed that at the time of introducing 'NEWALLOY', his father had accumulated a wide experience of thin wall pressure die casting via the production of typewriter bases and smaller parts.

** Four wheel sizes were not included in the Newalloy range, the 5/8" and 3/4" diameter bogie wheels, and the1.7/8" and 2.1/16" loco drivers. In 1937 these larger drivers were dropped from the product range. The bogie wheels were also dropped from the post war catalogues, but the ¾" wheel was re-introduced in Newalloy in 1952 to be fitted to the outside cylinder 4-4-0 freelance locomotives.

Describing Newalloy as an alloy of 'aluminium' was perhaps a copy writer's slip or a deliberate attempt to forestall competition. By 1935 however the alloy was correctly described as one of zinc and listed its strength as:

Tensile strength..............47,300 psi* (33.26 kg/mm²)
Compressive strength.....93,100 psi* (65.46 kg/mm²)

By 1935 the company was advertising its capacity to produce zinc castings for other applications, listing in the catalogue some two dozen 'trades' as potential users from the automotive to the wireless industry and inviting trade enquiries.

Use of Newalloy was progressively extended to other items. 'NON-LOK' oval head buffers were introduced in 1931. More significantly the frames and motor front bearing block of the new mechanisms for the standard tanks were designed for Newalloy, a measure which not only greatly simplified the units but significantly reduced the cost for production and final assembly. From the end of 1936, bogies for the Bakelite coaches and axleguards for the Bakelite wagons likewise were cast in Newalloy. After the war the change to a permanent magnet motor necessitated the fitting of a slender die cast backplate to carry the rear shaft bearing.

Unfortunately neither the zinc suppliers nor the operators of casting equipment of the day understood the essential requirement to keep the alloy pure and clean. The zinc used to create these simple alloys, usually with aluminium and copper, often contained small additions of lead, tin, or antimony, as an aid to fluidity. These impurities segregated to the grain boundaries of the zinc and castings thus affected would later begin to fail dramatically from intergranular corrosion, (see Glossary), this causing swelling, cracking and, in the worst cases, ultimate total disintegration. The practice of dropping faulty castings, flash and other 'dirty' metal back into the melting pot, no doubt deemed commendable in the interests of economy, also aggravated the situation and has left us with a terrible legacy of failures. Alongside these, however, stand the durable 'pure metal'** castings as stable and sharp as when they were first produced.

In the mid-1960s, cadmium plating was introduced for Newalloy loco wheels, which were then 'Guaranteed for 5 years against failure'! Failures there would surely have been, but the company was by then no longer in existence to honour the warranty. Of a few examples seen today and samples held in the Trust archive, exfoliation of the electroplate in addition to the familiar swelling and cracking, explains why very few of these wheels have survived.

*psi = pounds per square inch

**The international top industrial standard of purity for zinc is today 99.995%

14   Fire!

Rex Stedman remained owner of the LMC, trading under his own name, until August 1932. In this period of increasing unemployment and steadily falling prices the company was obviously struggling. Many of the advertisements offered items – particularly those which were slower selling, such as the 0-6-2 and 0-4-4 series I tank locos - at substantially reduced prices. In August the company released details of 'a serious fire' at the Jack Lane works which had occurred on Wednesday, June 29th, and which had caused a 'temporary' stoppage of work. The details reported in several of the local papers indicated that the fire had started in the spring room. Employees working there ran for sand, but on their return found that the flames had taken a firm hold and the Fire Brigade was called. By the time a first fire engine had arrived the two-storey brick building was completely ablaze. A second engine was called and eventually, with the aid of three jets from the street main, the fire was brought under control. The spring room was totally destroyed, the roof and floors of the building, fixtures and fittings and a large number of models were badly damaged. Speaking to the Yorkshire Evening Post George Simpson estimated the damage at around £3,000 (£140,000 at today's prices), a sum which would have enabled an effective if modest restoration and update in tools and equipment. Nine employees were temporarily out of work, but the hope was expressed to be back in business in less than a month.

In less than that month, Rex Stedman had surrendered his directorship and interest in the company to fellow directors Moore and Simpson. After restoring the name Leeds Model Company Ltd. they used the LMC initials to depict 'Leeds Models Continued'. Their first catalogue acknowledged the company as the 'late R.F. Stedman & Co. Ltd', and featured all items in the existing (Stedman) range. This even included the Stedman private owner wagon, despite what we now believe was the total or near total loss, due to water damage, of stock of several of the coach and wagon lithographs. The introduction in the next catalogue (1935) of new 1934 coach style for the GWR steel sided 'button logo' coaches, and the total absence of the preceding panelled GW coaches with the London and Bristol shields emblem suggests that these at least were a total loss. One year later the catalogue listing of SR coaches and the SR open wagon were overprinted 'Temporarily out of stock' but neither the wagon nor the coaches re-appeared in the catalogue for the following year, (1937) from which the bogie open wagons and the NE bogie box van were also withdrawn. It is of course possible to speculate that these items were casualties of slower sales, but in all cases no litho papers have survived, whereas papers from other pre-grouping stock and LMS, LNER and GW button logo papers were among the stocks sold off in the liquidation sales in 1966. Unused original papers of most of these items are held in the Trust archive. The conclusion has to be that there were genuine losses of litho papers in the fire, although no specific details of the losses are available.

The fire coming when it did has caused a few sceptical commentators to suggest that it was started for the convenience of the company. An insurance claim on ageing, slow moving stock and outdated machinery would certainly enable regeneration and re-investment to update both products and manufacturing equipment. The Jack Lane factory was old, the picture below shows a typically

cluttered and untidy corner of the workshop, where fires or other accidents might occur at any time. Work in progress would have been backed up with stocks of paper, glues, timber, paints and solvents. Other readily combustible materials would include wood shavings and sawdust, oily rags and the like, and these might well have been close to where the fire started, but there was no evidence found to suggest foul play. The reports at the time clearly indicate that the fire started accidentally and no one today can prove this or disprove it.

The fact remains that the company survived the fire and emerged to continue, with the development and manufacture its most lasting and iconic products: the second series of standard tanks and the range of Bakelite coaches vans and wagons.

15　　　Nettle and the Brighton Belle

The Sentinel steam railcar 'Nettle' (DVD 68) was the last model designed in detail by Rex Stedman in 1931, before he left the company in 1932. The evidence of his hand is present on the vehicle's solebar strip which carries the date, 5/10/30, and a square plate on which the then company title R.F. Stedman & Co was to have been printed.

Instead 'LMC' in small white letters, to which name the company reverted in September 1932', took its place. Clearly preparation for production of the railcar substantially overran the original schedule. The model was entirely new. The all-timber bodywork (profiled roof and ends with flat sides and floor) and the striking green and cream lithographs were all ready in 1931 and were much less of a problem than the new motor bogie. The main delay appears to have been due to

attempts to provide a battery driven model, with batteries carried inside the hollow interior of the timber body. (The motor bogie is attached with a 4 BA screw through the roof into the magnet. The recess for the screw is concealed by the coal chute cover). In the event the model powered by third rail current collection was finally released for sale in August 1933 with apologies for the delay. The battery powered option was admitted to be 'indefinitely delayed' owing to the inability of battery makers to come up with a small enough battery of sufficient power and durability. Following the introduction of Nettle the company, in time for Christmas 1934, launched the five car 'Brighton Belle' set, with motor bogies in the end cars, 88 and 89. (The motor bogie was attached by a large press stud mounted on the top of the magnet to a mating stud attached to the inside of the coach roof). From 1939 onwards the die cast bogies were fitted to the rake with a suitable adaptation to the motor bogie (see Appendix B)

True to prototype, the trailing cars were first class 'Hazel' and 'Doris', and third class car No. 86. From the late 1940s the Pullman lithographs were also printed without numbers or names respectively so that owners could customize their own rakes, in some cases using only non-motor units for a steam-hauled train.

16   Renaissance - Standard Tank Engines II

Back in 1927, Rex Stedman had built a model of the GC Class 3 (LNER F1) 2-4-2T which had convincingly demonstrated the incorporation of an electric mechanism into a low profile boiler model (DVD 80). The reviewer, in the June issue of Model Railway News, was obviously impressed by the small diameter of the boiler. It was emphasised that the locomotive could only be supplied with electric drive, *'it being impossible to get a clockwork mechanism into so small a space'*. The locomotive, now in the keeping of the Trust, proved to be the genesis of a second range of tank locomotives. These six equally small boilered models were selected from prototypes of the LNER, LMS and SR. As with the Series I tanks, each body was to be produced from a single set of tools but each frame, irrespective of wheel numbers and spacing was to be pressure die cast from a single set of dies and inserts. For all the similarities suggested by this economical approach, each locomotive was nonetheless different from each of the others in an individual way. Varied overall lengths and wheel arrangements were further matched with combinations of other parts, chimneys, domes etc. (see Appendix E)

Lack of money again delayed the introduction of the new models. Only after Rex Stedman's departure from the LMC in 1932, did George Simpson, acknowledged to be one of the best production engineers in the model business, start to plan the details for production. The manufacture of sheet metal tooling, dies for pressure die casting in 'Newalloy' and other tools, followed by prototype manufacture and testing, took in all a further two years. In June 1935 and almost immediately before the release of the range, the company moved to larger premises in Potterdale Mills. Finally in September 1935 and in a new catalogue, the range of six locomotives was finally released. What a sensation these must have created! If we judge by the numbers still in existence they must have outsold almost all other quality models available at the time. The two largest models of the series, and perhaps for this reason the most popular were the LMS (ex L & Y) 2-4-2T (DVD 81) and the LNER (Ex GC) 0-6-2T (DVD 82). The other locos were an LMS (also ex L & Y) 0-6-2T (DVD 83), an SR (Ex L&SWR) 0-4-4T (DVD 84), an LNER (Ex GE) 2-4-2T (DVD 85), and (nowadays the hardest to find) an LNER (EX GE) 0-4-4T (DVD 86). Other than the SR loco which was turned out in lined malachite green, the other five were black with red lining, all as shown below and on page 50, over.

0-4-4
G.E. 8120 Class

Cat. No.:
   A.C. LA/10.
   D.C. LD/10.

2-4-2
G.E. Class F.4.

Cat. No.
   A.C. LA/11.
   D.C. LD/11.

0-6-2
G.C. No. 5773.

Cat. No.
   A.C. LA/12.
   D.C. LD/12.

The full range continued to be available for a short time after the war. However, by 1948 when the locos again appeared in the catalogue, the LNER 0-4-4T had gone to be replaced by an 0-6-0T (DVD 87) available in LMS and LNER plain black and SR green liveries. The 0-6-0T and the LNER 0-6-2T were also offered in LNER green fully lined out, but as bodies only. Additionally, sets of parts for construction of the locos were sold free of purchase tax, and at one stage the company offered a prize for the best kit built loco to encourage modellers and enthusiasts to this lower cost route to their hobby. By the early 1950's the LNER 2-4-2T was phased out, the five remaining models continuing up to the end of the decade when John Potter took over the company (by then trading as Ellemsee Accessories), and re-moved them from the product range.

Good as they are, the models are by no means perfect. Pre-treatment of the tinplate bodies prior to painting was their weakness. Poor paint adhesion has led to flaking and in some cases rusting of the exposed metal. The cure is to strip, de-rust and repaint. All of these models were hand painted in the factory, so reproducing the

0-6-2 L.M.S.
(L. & Y.).

Cat No.:
A.C. LA/20·
D.C. LD/20.

2-4-2 L.M.S.
(L. & Y.).
Horwich Rebuild.

Cat. No.:
A·C. LA/21
D.C. LD/21

0-4-4 S.R.
(L.S.W.R.).

Adams Class
T.1.
Ex. No. 3.

Cat. No.:
A.C. LA/22.
D.C. LD/22.

process with modern materials in order both to preserve the models and to enhance the pleasure in their use is strongly encouraged. More serious in terms of operating the locomotives was the progressive deterioration of the zinc alloy wheels, frames and motor parts (see Newalloy Chapter 13). Here the cure may be restoration if parts are available or the installation of an entirely new mechanism.

Today examples of the series can be found often in substantially original condition, sometimes modified, in many collections or running on many layouts. It is a tribute to Stedman's original concept of versatility within a standardised format that these locomotives continue to please and be admired wherever they are encountered.

17   Bakelite

Bakelite, the first 'plastic', was invented in the first decade of the last century (see Glossary). Its usefulness and versatility was soon established in a wide range of applications: engineering, electrical, domestic and decorative. In 1935, LMC experimented with coloured Bakelite to produce moulded open wagons and box vans. The results were quite outstanding, the finished products rivalling the best hand built models available for accuracy, strength and appearance. The models were launched in 1937.

12-ton Standard Mineral Wagon.

A range of colours were used for the 12-ton mineral drop end wagons: red oxide or dark lead grey for the LNER (NE) (DVD 88), brown for the S.R, bauxite for the LMS, and dark lead grey for the GWR (DVD 89). In perhaps a modest attempt to understate the realism for the models the company accepted that the only thing wrong with the models is 'that the door will not drop'!

The pre-1940 vans, LMS and LNER, were similarly varied in livery colours, with the addition of passenger lake for an LMS fish van. Initially van roofs were white, but varied browns and greys were introduced later. Roof ventilators and brake pipes were added where appropriate. The company making many claims for these models stated that the vans were, 'so realistic that many people have tried to slide the door'! (DVD 90, 91).

True Scale Freight Van.

Following this success the company moved to produce coaches, a mottled brown and yellow for the LNER teak effect (DVD 92 93), red for the LMS (DVD 94) and green for the SR (DVD 95). The 'chocolate and cream' GW coaches were moulded in brown and painted cream above the waistline (DVD 96). Pre-1940 coaches and goods vehicles are thus easily identified by their self colour.

After 1945, when only black Bakelite was available, all stock was painted in an appropriate livery. The inability to paint the LNER teak finish meant the end of the line for that rail-way. After the formation of British Railways, in 1948 'blood and custard' coaches were offered (DVD 97). All the coaches were shorter by one window than a standard length vehicle, allowing

3rd Class Vestibule Brake Composite.

them to traverse 3ft radius curves. Production was limited to two types: a third class vestibule coach and a third class vestibule brake composite. Pre-war mould-ings are very slightly shorter than the post-war versions, probably because new moulds were made. Pre- and post-war roofs are thus not interchangeable. Roofs on the first coaches supplied were not secured other than by gravity and a gentle push-fit against the ends of the coaches. If the roofs fell off with the coach inverted the glazing glass would drop out of the window side slots. The remedy applied was a cranked rod, the short end of which was passed through a drilled hole in the central roof brace and the lower end, which was threaded, secured with a washer and nut through the coach floor. Although the company claimed that the models were 'impervious to climatic conditions' distortion is evident today on some models as the probable result of excessive heating (sunlight outdoors or through windows, especially where the railway is in a green house etc). The rod securing the roof may be used with care to limit and correct such distortion.

Despite its shortcomings, Bakelite enabled LMC to reproduce a wealth of detail on the moulded coach bodies, handrails, steps, dummy electric cable fittings, carriage door handles, hinges and step boards etc. The removable roof gave access to the interior for additional detailing by the owners if desired. Bakelite is an insulator and wiring for coach lighting could be easily fitted. Sockets for small light bulbs and slots for wiring were moulded into the underside of the roofs. Suitable miniature lamps were supplied by the company if required, but installation, and suggested interior detailing, was left to the individual modeller.

The pressure die cast Newalloy bogies wheels and 'NON-LOK' buffers were standard for the coach range. Other non-Bakelite parts were the wooden battery box, the brass truss rods, the upper ends of which were held in the heads of split pins secured in the coach floor, the card and fabric corridor connectors, standard three link couplings, white metal roof vents, (torpedo for the LNER coaches, but shell vents for all others) and the glazing. The glass used for glazing was 1mm thick and before the war was supplied from Czechoslovakia. After the war stocks ran down and supplies were erratic. Many coaches were glazed with clear plastic sheet. Glass (0.8mm thick) from 35mm slides and cut to size is successfully used in Bakelite coach restorations carried out by the Trust.

The LMC catalogues of 1952 and 1953 included six pages detailing the use of LMC wagon and van bodies for free lance modelling. The article, with sketches

and photographs of finished models, two of which are shown here, was supplied by Cyril Dixon. In the 'Leeds Lines' article in the Gauge '0' Guild Gazette (Vol.11 No. 1 December 1989), it was wrongly stated that 'these models were all produced for Cyril Dixon'. Almost immediately Cyril wrote from his home in Whangarei, New Zealand, to confirm that he was the builder, the only LMC contribution being the black Bakelite body mouldings. I was pleased to visit Cyril in 2006 and see these fine models on his layout. I was also able to reassure him that the error in respect of their creator would not be repeated!

Rather belatedly in following up on these clever adaptations of the basic Bakelite mouldings, from 1964 onwards the company offered coach body mouldings 'only while existing stocks last' and with the added note: *'The moulding dies for these coaches have been destroyed and these units cannot be repeated. We are advised by a prominent member* of the Gauge '0' Guild that these coaches, if 3 are bought, can be cut to make two 'bang on' scale units. Alternatively, if you are not too worried about scale to length, these mouldings are the basis of a very attractive job'.*

To support the range of Bakelite wagons and vans a better goods brake van other than the old litho models was required. With the introduction of the Bakelite goods stock in 1937 the company released three hand built brake vans, LMS, LNER and SR, painted in bauxite, red oxide and SR brown respectively (DVD 98). These vans closely matched prototypes operating on the different railways at the time. The LNER version pictured here was, as the others, built with wooden roof and sides mounted on a steel base.The models both before and after the war were only available assembled and finished. This was an entirely logical development, for whilst it was financially viable to create injection moulds for hundreds of entirely standard wagons and vans, such was not the case for the individually styled brake vans which would in any event sell in far fewer numbers. After the war only the LMS model was continued, but manufactured in tinplate. Initially lettered 'LMS' this was changed to 'M' for BR Midland Region after nationalisation. In 1950 a further version of the model was issued but sold separately, primarily to go with the goods train set. This was also made from tinplate and similar in appearance to the standard LMS brake van, but was shorter, 5.1/8 inches, (130mm), across the buffer beams as compared to 6.11/16 inches, (170mm), for the standard vehicle, (DVD 99). A moulded resin model of the long wheel base van is held in the archive. This replicates the dimensions of the LMC model, and may have been a private venture by an independent modeller rather than an attempt by the company to economise by moving from hand building the tinplate vans to less labour intensive assembly of a fully moulded vehicle.

*Reported to have been the late Ken Leeming

18   Exhibitions

Throughout the years from 1912 Rex Stedman regularly sought opportunities to exhibit the products and capabilities of his company. The records show that his first display layout, (pictured below), an electrified 15 ft x 5ft double track circuit with sidings and passing loops, was provided for the Christmas 1913 window show for Boolds, a large department store in Devonport. No record exists of the locomotives or stock used.

The effusive letter of thanks from Boolds commented on *'the special efforts put forward by their engineer, Mr. Steadman* (sic) *who has been untiring in his successful endeavours whilst setting up the model railway in working order'.*

No less complimentary is the March 1915 letter to Rex from Mason's, a Bradford photographic store. They had purchased a layout, locos and rolling stock which, *'...were working all day long during a period of five weeks, and during that time we had not a single moments trouble..'* Somewhat amusingly the writer notes, *'..the models were a great advertisement, the only drawback was that at times we had to draw the blinds so that people would clear away from the windows'* !

The first post-war Model Engineering Exhibition was held in 1922. The company took the space allocated to four stands, the main part of which was taken up by the model railway pictured below. Access to the central operating area of the layout was via the fully working Scherzer bridge shown here. Behind the layout, were

display shelves for models, track formations and accessories. This was the first major opportunity the company had to show off the extent and quality of its product range. Perhaps the most surprising element was that the locomotives were all clockwork drive, a test of the operators' endurance as well as that of the locos themselves – the 1 in 48 gradient up to the goods yard representing a regular challenge!

The British Empire Exhibition at Wembley was opened in 1924 and proved so popular that it remained open until October 1925. The existing Model Engineering Exhibition layout which had also been displayed at the same event in 1923 was electrified for the BE Exhibition. The LMC stand was located in the Palace of Housing and Transport (opposite to the GWR Pendennis Castle). Advertising the layout in the September 1925 issue of Model Railway News, Stedman claimed,

'This electric model railway is the most complete Gauge 0 system that has ever been exhibited'. Three trains could be run simultaneously, two on the main running ovals, one on shunting in the goods yard. All sections of the layout were signalled and interlocked.

The layout features briefly in the official film 'Wembley 1925'. In 1948, Peter Baylis produced a film, 'The Peaceful Years', the theme of which was to contrast the starkness of life at the time *'real life'*, with the various forms of escapism pursued in the 1920s and 1930s. One of the scenes depicted, (for 1925), was the LMC Wembley model railway with Rex Stedman himself at the controls. The commentator passed the remark, *'and we even had time for model railways!'*.

At the close of the Wembley exhibition the layout shown here returned to Leeds, where, on November 28th, it was displayed at The Grand Pygmalion. The event was opened by the Lord Mayor of Leeds who was presented with an LNER Director carrying his name 'John Arnott' and numbered with the year 1925 (see also Chapter 9). The railway was filmed on the day by Gaumont Graphic Film News Network initially purely for local interest but it was later shown in cinemas nationally during the week commencing the 7th of December - just in time for Christmas. The January 1926 issue of Model Railway news reported *'...very large crowds are flocking to see the model every day and at each demonstration explanatory remarks are made with a view to helping the uninitiated to understand the manoeuvres though which the locomotives and trains are put...'*

Following on from the move to Leeds the layout was moved to Blackpool where it was on display from 1926 to 1937*. Thomas Hargreaves wrote to me in 1993 with his recollections, as a young lad of thirteen, of the layout at the Pleasure Beach on the South Shore at Blackpool, The layout, set behind several tiers of tip-up chairs, was housed in a small pavilion in the heart of the fairground near to the Fun House and was under the direction of Captain E.C. Ball, *'a fine smart gentleman with a small military moustache. He was an enthusiast through and through and very proud of all the products'.* Arrangement of the layout was identical to the Wembley scheme but with the addition of a loop line from the outer track which ran to an external showcase. Every now and again a train would travel along the loop to show itself off to those outside in the hope that they would pay their sixpences (2½p) and come inside. As at Wembley, the layout power was 8 volts and all the vehicles had automatic couplings. Locomotives running were the LNER 4-6-0 'Sir Sam Fay' and 4-4-0 'Butler Henderson'. The goods engine was the Pickersgill 0-6-0 and yard shunting was carried out by the ubiquitous 0-4-0 saddle tank.

Advertisements in MRN from 1926 onwards point to a busy round of exhibitions for the LMC. In August 1926, the company reported on the show they had put on for the tercentenary of the city of Leeds in the Industrial Exhibition in the Town Hall, and announced its plans for the Model Engineering Exhibition in September.

In his letter to his wife, (to whom he was 'Billy'), on New Year's Eve, 1926, Rex was anything but happy about the next show, the Schoolboy's Exhibition at the Horticultural Hall. *'I find'*, he wrote, *'we have a great barn of a stand and also there is practically nothing to go on it. I have not a single loco up here yet – (the show opened on January 1st) – and I foresee a rotten show altogether. However I am really writing to wish you a Very Happy New Year and to hope we shall see many more together and more prosperous ones'.*

The LMC stand at the 1927 Model Engineering Exhibition featured static displays only and the emphasis, not surprisingly for the time, was on product sales. Understandably the MEE was missed with the upheavals of September 1928, but Stedman, by then trading under his own name, was back in 1929, introducing his new range of post-grouping coaches and wagons, and Newalloy wheels. The extended Newalloy parts range was on show for the MEE in 1930.

Recognising the significant role of Bonds O' Euston Road as sales agents for the company, Stedman used their stand exhibition to display and sell his product range. This arrangement with Bonds was used again at the Model Engineering

*see also Gauge '0' Guild Gazette March 1994 Vol. 12, No 6, pp 206 - 208

Exhibition in 1931, the 'attraction' being further price reductions on all products and especially on slower moving items such as the 0-6-2 and 0-4-4 series 1 standard tanks.

For the Model Railway Club Exhibition in 1931 Rex displayed his 25 ft (7.6m) model of the Sydney Harbour Bridge. The bridge had moving vehicles, and sunrise/sunset effects by means of dimmer controlled coloured lighting in the diorama. He also included the commercial demonstration models of Green's scraper tube and diamond pattern economisers.

Despite the fire and the departure of Rex Stedman the company put on a brave face and exhibited at the MEE again in 1932. The annual MEE show was attended again in 1933 and in each subsequent year until 1939, when, with apologies advertised in Model Railway News, they limited themselves to display stands to show off samples of the Bakelite brake composite coach mouldings which had been introduced earlier in the year.

No records exist either in the Model Railway News or elsewhere to suggest that the company participated directly in any further exhibitions. In the post war period the focus was on appointing sales agents and if any of those chose to exhibit, LMC products would inevitably have been displayed. This was possibly deemed to be a satisfactory as well as an economic way to deal with exhibiting in general and at the Model Engineering Exhibitions in particular. Little wonder that model railway enthusiasts progressively became less and less aware of the company and ultimately became less likely buyers of its products.

19   Austerity and afterwards

Staying in the model railway business, particularly in 0 Gauge in the years immediately following the end of World War II, was a struggle to say the least. Not only was there a shortage of all materials, but costs for those which could be purchased were double what they had been in 1939. Higher costs for labour and overheads were further aggravated by purchase tax. Wealthy customers were fewer and farther between and so increasing efforts were made to sell off all surplus materials and essentially redundant stock.

The catalogues from 1946 onwards give no details of the directors of the company. The last mention of R.S. Moore is as a participant with the 'great and the good' of the model industry, at the creation of M.E.T.A. (Model Engineering Trade Association) at Kings Cross in January 1945. Thereafter LMC adverts (and those of many other model engineering companies) carried the META badge. It seems likely that Moore left the company and Mr. R. Rathbone, a retired teacher and apparently a model builder in his own right, took the lead. George Simpson, a very fine production engineer, most probably served as Works Manager, and H.C. Bradley was certainly Distribution Manager. These three then shouldered the workaday burdens.

Taking an early initiative, probably Bradley's, to reduce pressure on the limited number of staff running the company, LMC announced that customers in the UK should in future make use of the company's local agents, rather than contacting the Potterdale Mills factory as had been the case in the past. Twenty two new agents were appointed in 1946, these in addition to the forty or so which already covered the country. London alone now had seven outlets, two of which were in the City! The national emphasis on exporting was reflected by the LMC in appointing more agents to cover their overseas markets.

Information provided by Bruce Macdonald confirms that Rathbone visited Japan in 1948, although the purpose of the visit to find a supplier - or less likely a distributor - is unclear. *En route* Rathbone called in to see the owner of Fleet Trains in Sydney, Gordon Usherwood. Again, no records exist to indicate the purpose of the visit, but Rathbone had brought with him sufficient 'Metalway' track to make up an oval layout with a central crossover. He left this with Usherwood but the track was never unpacked and eventually, via the author, came back to the UK in 2010.

For the LMC, committed to moulded Bakelite stock, the inability to obtain sufficient supplies was a serious blow. The Bakelite coaches for example did not reappear in the catalogue until 1948 and then were designated for export only. Coach mouldings (untrimmed) were available in a limited quantity for the home market. Customers for coaches in the interim period were offered sets of wooden coach parts with a choice of papers other than SR.

In 1948, with the ongoing supply problem of Bakelite unresolved, the company produced a 'Rigid litho' coach (DVD 100). This used the LMS suburban coach lithograph printed onto a single sheet of stiff black card which was shaped with a curved roof and flat sides turned under to fit onto a thick block of wood which formed the floor. The window apertures were punched out and glazed with celluloid film. The coach ends were zinc die castings, attached to the floor with screws. The coach as a ready to run item was fitted with the pressure die cast bogies, 'NON-LOK' buffers and other standard LMC fittings. These somewhat ungainly models rather vaguely described appeared only twice in the catalogues for 1946 and 1947 but otherwise received scant publicity. As shown above, they were supplied both as finished models and kits. Although cast ends with windows were produced for a brake composite coach, no examples have been found. By 1947 the supply of Bakelite began to ease and the rigid litho concept was quietly dropped. Swelling and cracking of the cast zinc alloy ends is a familiar problem for the relative few of these models which have survived.

The drive for lower cost products saw the introduction of a standard 4-4-0 tender locomotive - described by many as a cut-down version of the earlier Director. Initially produced as an inside cylinder model (DVD 101), an outside cylinder version (DVD 102) followed, along with the outside cylinder version of the 0-4-0 saddle tank already described. The 4-4-0 was accompanied in the catalogue by one further standard 0-6-0 tank loco, (DVD 87). One may wonder about the numbering of these freelance models. Adrian Stedman advised that it was standard practice to choose numbers for the engines of the various classes which would use up all the figures on the transfer sheets! The 4-4-0, 0-4-0ST and 0-6-0T models were offered in every livery and also as kits. Purchase tax chargeable on finished models was a significant part of the cost at the time. (Kits were purchase tax free.) The company promoted 'build-it-yourself' by offering an annual prize of £10 for the best kit built locomotive. A promotional letter of 1947 detailed the three second series tank locomotives which were then supplied in kit form: the new LMS 0-6-0, the LNER 0-6-2, and the LMS 2-4-2. The models had to be built to the drawing supplied and only from parts manufactured by LMC. Any additional detailing or the inclusion of 'foreign parts' would disqualify the entry. Models entered for the competition were not to be painted – no hiding up of badly soldered joints! – but they could be given a coat of clear varnish to prevent rusting. Although professional model makers were barred from participation, modellers under 18 were encouraged to enter with age being taken into account by the judges in awarding a further prize of £10. The first prize winners were announced in the July 1948 issue of Model Railway News.

From the early 1950s using outworkers the company offered models of the LMS Jubilee, (DVD 103), the GW 4-6-0 Hawksworth County, (DVD 104), the LMS

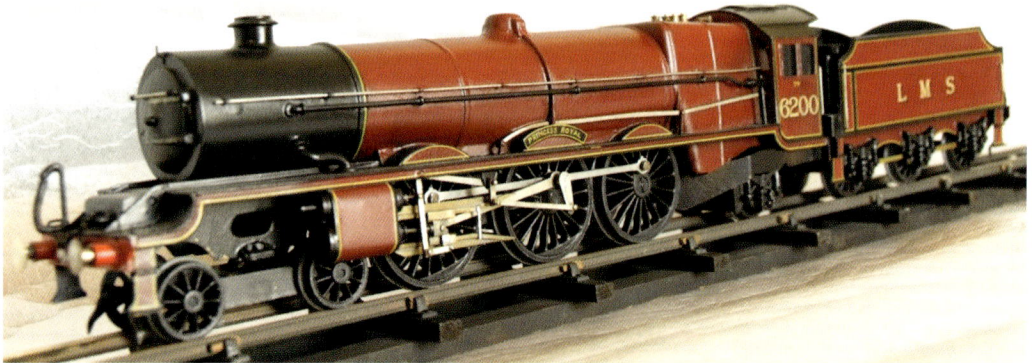

Princess pictured here, a GW 0-6-0 Pannier tank (shown over) and 2-6-2 Prairie tanks. Available along with items in the standard range up to the end of the 1950s these were particularly fine models, but skill and standards between the different builders means that models often differ one to the next. Several examples today are fitted with other than LMC mechanisms, possibly at the request of the original buyers, or by later replacement of the LMC motor unit.

For a short time from April 1952 the company initiated the 'L.M.C. '0' Gauge Club'*. For an agreed fee of £30.00 paid at £1.00 per week, members would be entitled to a discount of 10% on the list prices. (Smaller fees of £15.00 – 10 shillings (50p) per week and £5.00 – 5 shillings (25p) per week earned discounts of 5% and 2½% respectively). The rather complicated rules and conditions may well have made the system unattractive to would be buyers. No further records exist of the scheme.

Although the focus of the company from 1946 onwards was on '0' gauge, it remained willing to undertake commissions to build models in other gauges. One very fine example is the 1" to 1 foot model (1/12 scale), 3.1/4" (82.5mm) gauge scale model of the 2-8-4T locomotive No 3 built by their Leeds neighbour Hudswell Clarke & Co Ltd. for IPC, the Iraq Petroleum Co Ltd. No 3 and its

two sisters are described in Ron Redman's book 'The Railway Foundry, Leeds' as 'the ultimate steam locomotives' of Hudswell Clarke & Co. This model, pictured left, was built by LMC in the early 1950s and placed on display in the entrance hall of the main Hudswell Clarke office block. It is now in the care of the Middleton Railway Trust.

*Not to be confused with the Leeds Model Railway Club which for a time held its meetings at LMC's Potterdale Mills factory . R. Rathbone was President of the Club in 1947. Ronald Ellis of LMC was acting Secretary.

'A worthy present for a Worthy Son': thus in 1949 did the Leeds Model Company introduce their first ever boxed train set. This comprised an 0-4-0 loco, two Bakelite box vans, one Bakelite open wagon and a single 15ft (4.5m) oval of track, all packed neatly in a brown leatherette presentation box. Various plans for enlarged layouts were depicted on the inside of the box lid.

A worthy present for a
Worthy Son

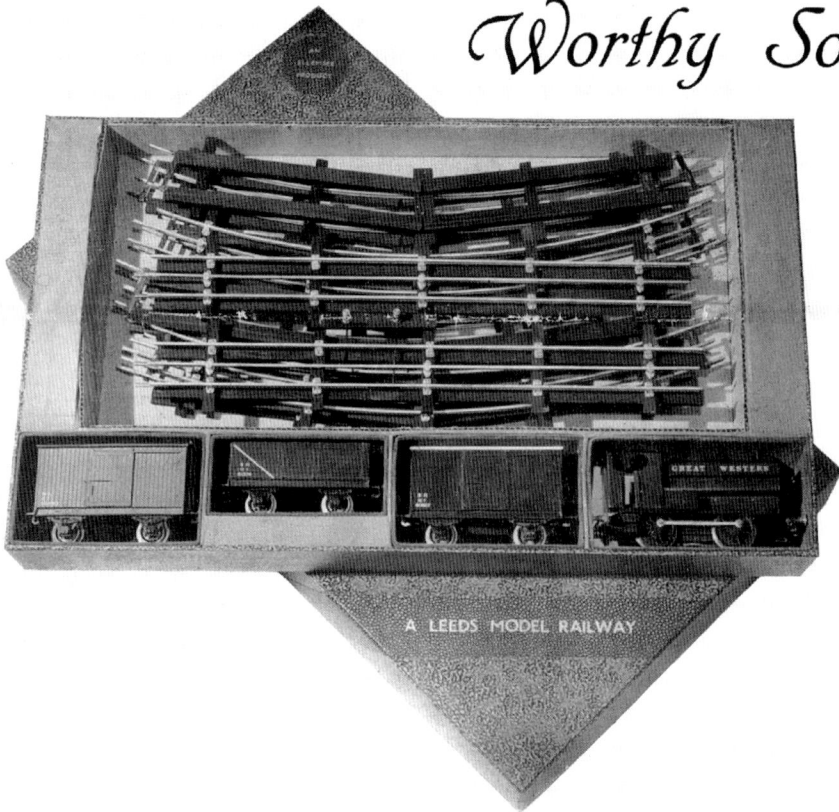

A LEEDS MODEL RAILWAY

The set was 'comprehensively guaranteed for one year'. The three rail (centre third) track was made up of eight 2ft 1.1/2" (.65m) radius 'Metalway' curves and two 18" (.45m) straight sections, one of which carried connectors for the power source – which was not supplied. The set with a locomotive without smoke apparatus was priced at a twelve pounds, four shillings and five pence (£12.22).

The odd amount reflected the effect of purchase tax! The smoke unit if fitted added one pound ten shillings and seven pence to this, the set price then totalling thirteen pounds fifteen shillings (£13.75). The early sets were supplied with inside cylinder locos with liveries of one or other of the big four companies and wagons to match. Later, the outside cylinder 0-4-0ST (DVD 6) in BR livery was substituted, but the wagons remained with the original transfer liveries and numbers.

Passenger train sets were also available in big four and BR liveries. These contained a post war 4-4-0 tender locomotive with three Bakelite coaches but rather crammed as they were into a goods set box, ('Goods' deleted and 'Passenger' handwritten), they were sold without track.

Paradoxically, no mention of the 0-4-0ST or either goods or passenger train sets appears in the otherwise comprehensive 1952 and 1953 catalogues, the last

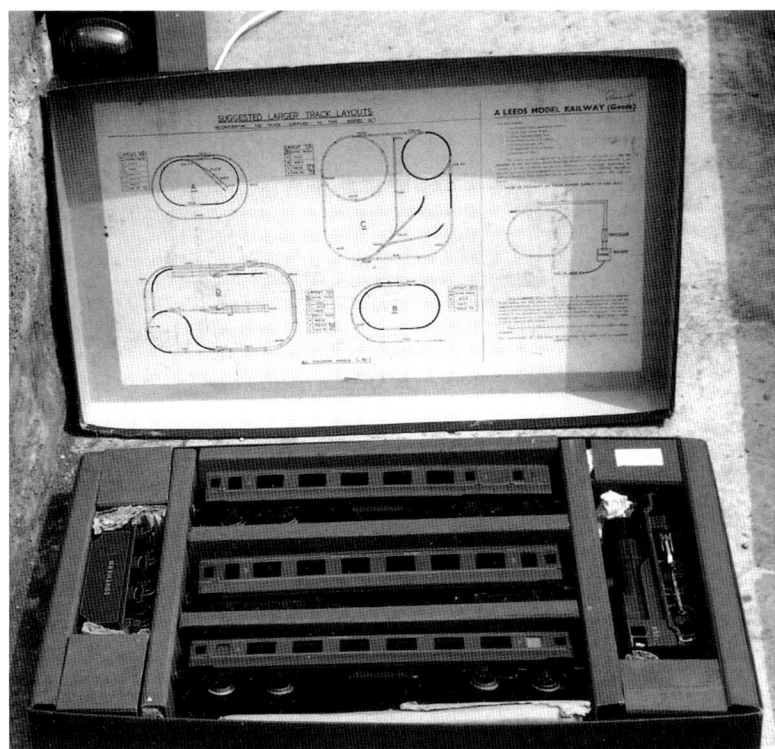

publications of high quality produced by LMC; neither was there any mention of the sets in the price lists issued in 1957, 1959, and through the 60s up to the 1967 liquidation.

A significant number of boxed sets in various states of preservation appear to have survived to the present, but no record can be found as to how many and of what type were ever sold. The number would certainly have been small in relation to Hornby Trains. Despite the 'worthy' LMC objective of promoting wider sales, and a series of advertisements in the Meccano Magazine, the higher price of the LMC sets would have been just as much a deterrent to purchase as for other Leeds products.

21   The Sincerest Form of Flattery!

Imitation, proverbially the sincerest form of flattery, has dogged many manufacturers across a wide range of engineering products; no less so for the model railway business.

Copies of Leeds Model Company locomotives and rolling stock date from the 1930s when the Japanese company Seki (or Sakai), supplied the UK market with a range of '0' gauge products under the name 'Stronlite'. Amongst these was a model of the Leeds 0-4-0 saddle tank, the difference most readily visible being the sandboxes, the high sides of which were required to enclose the armature of the electric motor which was placed across the width of the model. The final drive from the motor was to spur gears which formed the flanges of the driving wheels on one side of the locomotive. Other models resembling LMC products were a GC 4-6-0 'Sir Sam Fay', which was also supplied painted in LMS red and named 'Sir Gilbert Claughton' and Brighton Belle Pullman coaches which were not paper litho on wood, but tin printed, bearing the names 'Doris' and 'Evadne'. Printed tinplate copies of the LMS suburban litho coach No. 3395 and LNER coaches 2253, 38295 and 3627 were close to exact copies. The coach bogies however were of the 'American' type and made up from tinplate pressings rather than having any white metal cast parts. Tin printed open wagons bearing NE, LMS or SR lettering, on inspection prove to be blends of the LMC designs for the GW and NE post-grouping lithographs. Box vans and brake vans, similarly lettered for the big four are copies of the LMS box van and LMS brake van.

The question frequently asked about Stronlite is, "Are these copies, or was there collaboration between the LMC and Seki which permitted the production of these models in Japan?" Willem J.J. Boot, a leading authority on Japanese producers and their models, is quite clearly convinced that there was never any relationship between Seki (post war name Sakai) and British manufacturers. The remarkable similarity of fittings on the 0-4-0ST to LMC products could be explained by direct copying, or by the possibility of the Stronlite office in London acting as a purchasing agent for the Japanese company. At the time LMC would have been only too willing to introduce another revenue stream without deliberately wishing to arm a competitor, irrespective of the end-use of the products. Collaboration with the LMC is additionally considered to be less likely in the light of other Stronlite models including locomotives of close appearance to the Hornby 0-4-0T, the Milbro 4-4-2T and many other European and American makes.

Concurrently with Leeds, Milbro in the 1930s supplemented their wagon range with four lower cost paper litho on wood open wagons. These were in the liveries of the big four and priced at 3 shillings (15p) each and were half the price of their standard wooden wagons, but 3d (1.25p) more than their Leeds counterparts. Milbro papers were supplied in one wrap around piece rather than, as the LMC papers, in separate sections. The Milbro lithographs were certainly not copies of the LMC prints; the sharp-eyed have noted that the Milbro GW open wagon is numbered 109451, the LMC number is 109458, but the similarity ends there!

The widest range of litho papers for coaches and goods stock was provided from the mid 1930s by Merco (The Miniature Exhibition Railways Company) of Dundee. The range which started with papers for buildings, served both 00 and 0 gauge enthusiasts. The papers were, by report, printed at the same press already used by LMC. In the March and April 1933 issues Model Railway News LMC briefly offered litho papers for 00 gauge, which were presumably identical to those being offered at the time by Merco.

Much later, in the 1950s, Douglas Models (Douglas Brittain*) produced litho papers in NE bauxite for an 0 gauge open wagon and box van. The open wagon paper was also used with silk-screen overprinting to provide a private owner wagon 'Lovering & Pochin'. A few of the NE models and papers survive today but, by Brittain's admission in a letter to Adrian Stedman in 1980, the private owner *"didn't sell so as you could notice it!"*

Rex Stedman's original concept of using embossed card for wagon sides was re-introduced in the late 1960s by D.L. Cutts of Weston-super-Mare, trading as Domascelles, who for a time sold an impressive range of open wagon private owner liveries, many of which on models, and as unused cards, are still around today.

In 2009 Darstaed Vintage Trains acquired original sets of the lithographs of the Brighton Belle set from the Leeds Stedman Trust and, with Trust agreement, to the use of the art work and the layout of these and other LMC lithographs, have produced a fine range of printed tinplate models.

*Douglas Brittain also considered purchase of all or part of the LMC operation in 1964

Working together from the early 2000s with a skilled woodworker, Bruce Palmer and John Davies contrived to produce copies of LMC bodies for the 12" litho coach range, and other models including coaches for the 'Brighton Belle', goods wagons, various brake vans and the petrol tanker.

Working from his home and with skilful cutting and splicing of the LMC lithos, Simon Chambers has produced under the header of 'Beyond Leeds', a wide range of different Pullman coaches, a short coach in matching livery to be hauled by the Sentinel rail car 'Nettle', and a model of the articulated railcar 'Phenomena'. He continues to develop the concept, producing new models every year.

Pictured below is the Brighton Belle Pullman car 'Jack the Station Cat', custom made for Alan Cliff by Darstaed, using re-mastered artwork based closely on the original Leeds Model Company lithographs. The model was specially commissioned to celebrate the tenth birthday of Alan's popular series of 'Jack the Station Cat' books.

It is much to the credit of Rex Stedman that his innovative designs and impeccable artwork, which were copied in concept and sometimes in detail from an early date in the life of the Leeds Model Company, continue to be used almost a century later to satisfy today's often more critical model railway enthusiasts.

22   Ellemsee

'Elemsee'(sic) was the original telegraphic address of the Leeds Model Company. Stedman changed this to 'Modelsted' when he ran the company under his own name and it remained thus until the end of the war. The word 'Ellemsee' first appears in the catalogue for 1947, possibly at the instigation of R. Rathbone and, although the LMC name dominates, the contents of the catalogue were described as 'Ellemsee Products'. Compare the letterhead below dated 1947, with that for 1961, also on a letter from Rathbone, on which under the revised name of 'Ellemsee Accessories' the letters 'L.M.C' are all but invisible!

TELEPHONE: LEEDS 24925   TELEGRAMS: LEEDS 24925

ELLEMSEE PRODUCTS

LEEDS MODEL COMPANY LIMITED.

MODEL RAILWAY ENGINEERS

POTTERDALE MILLS
DEWSBURY ROAD

LEEDS, 11

25th November, 1947.

Telephone 646140

ELLEMSEE ACCESSORIES
(L.M.C.)

MODEL ENGINEERS

WHEATON AVENUE, HALTON, LEEDS 15

Our Ref. No   Your Ref. No.

Attention Adrian.F.Stedman.

25th March 1961.

In 1948, the price list which accompanied the catalogue was headed 'Ellemsee '0' Gauge Model Railway Equipment'. This practice was continued to 1950. No mention of Ellemsee however appears in the new fully detailed catalogues published in 1952 from a new address opposite Potterdale Mills at 30 Dewsbury Road, the one time site of Stedman's Cinematographic Laboratory.* (A further move to 9a Dewsbury Road was made at the end of the year).

*Rathbone reported to Adrian Stedman that when the company moved across the road in 1951 they found in the basement a partly constructed automatic film development plant, with Rex's operating notes attached. This had remained untouched throughout the war and for the six years thereafter.

From early 1946 'Ellemsee Products' was on the headline of some but not all advertisements in the model press. Elsewhere the Leeds Model Company was described as 'makers of Ellemsee products'. Sales agencies, mainly model shops, which were being heavily promoted as the sources for products were uniformly described as 'Ellemsee Agents'. The advertisements for the 1952 catalogue carried a new combined Ellemsee and Leeds Model Co. logo, shown here, but this logo made no appearance in the catalogue itself!

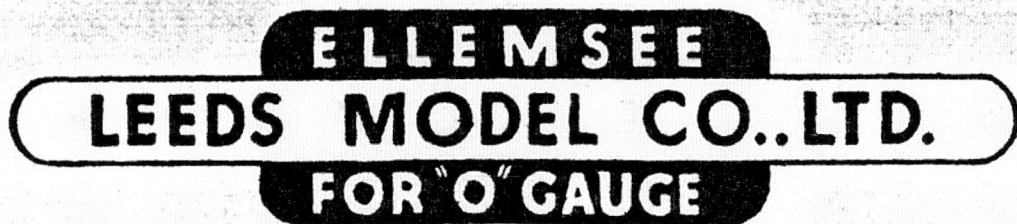

All the foregoing may seem rather trivial and irrelevant in the context of this book, but the muddled situation changed further in 1954 when Mr. C. A. Herring calling the company Ellemsee Accessories, advertised that he had *'purchased from the Leeds Model Company Ltd. the whole of their plant, tools and stock, and having engaged their staff of skilled workers, we are now producing the full range in-cluding articles not previously available since the war'*. A new catalogue was promised in the 1954 advertisement, but in the event the next publication in 1957 was a modest non-illustrated price list. This was issued from the company's 'new' premises in Wheaton Avenue Halton, (from where Stedman had first started the LMC in 1915). This list was more or less repeated in 1959.

In the absence of documentation, one is left to speculate on the position of Rathbone, as well as his relationship in the company or companies (LMC and Ellemsee) and with Herring. The problem is illustrated by information provided to the Trust in 1987 in regard to *'a locomotive, (Sir Sam Fay), that Mr. R. Rathbone of Ellemsee Accessories – Halton built for me in 1956'*. Writing to the author in 1986, the late Norman Green advised of his purchase in the 'mid 1950s' from LMC of an LNER 0-6-2T (series II) from Rathbone, *'who let me have it at trade price since he was selling out at the time'*, yet, in a letter to Green dated November 1965, Rathbone writes that he was *'in the throes of the action against Potter, to whom I sold Ellemsee Accessories'*. (Rathbone was awarded a judgement for the full amount owing and costs). In the same letter Rathbone discusses the dimensions and other features of Green's proposal for a model locomotive. *'In fact'*, reported Green, this locomotive was never built for me by Mr. Rathbone'

The exact time of arrival of John B. Potter on the LMC/Ellemsee scene is not clear from any information available to the Trust. In the early 1950s Potter was a small time sales-agent trading on commission and at times on his own account. He may well have become involved with Ellemsee at that time. In 1960 he incorporated his business and, as John B. Potter Ltd, traded as a light engineering company. The company letterhead advertised the product range as 'die casting, turning, light presswork, milling, sandblasting and finishing, and small electrical assemblies' – all of which typify facilities available within LMC and which were essential to their model railway manufacturing processes. In June 1964, Potter was facing a compulsory purchase order of his premises in central Leeds and purchasing Ellemsee Accessories from Rathbone, he moved his operations into the Ellemsee Wheaton Avenue plant.

Very soon, of the ten workers employed there only two were engaged on model railway work, the other eight on sub-contract projects. Potter perhaps not surprisingly if inadvisedly looked after the minority income from the railway business, leaving his works manager in charge of the sub-contact side of the business! His naivety in respect of model railways is clearly illustrated by his letter, written after *'a complete stock take at Wheaton Avenue'* and published in the September 1964 issue of Model Railway News: *'Being newcomers to the model engineering industry, the new owners of Ellemsee Accessories have been compelled to take an analytical look at the model railway market. Some comment that of the various gauges 0 is the smallest for detailed modelling purposes. Only a limited number of people seem to accept this and trade periodicals devote a large portion of space to narrow gauge, TT, 000 and 00 layouts and construction detail'.* He then suggested that with an *'exchange of correspondence in the MRN columns he might discover what enthusiasts and dealers really want'.* The Editor of MRN followed this letter with a cautionary note, suggesting that, *'those who would claim the earth for 0 gauge should refrain from expressing extreme ideas',* and that he hoped, *'only practical propositions for manufacturers and retailers would be forthcoming'.*

It would seem that no clear direction came from this appeal. Troubles mounted. Within a year Potter was accusing his works manager of failing to price work correctly and fired him, along with five of the workforce. In May and again in November 1966, the company was given generous publicity in Model Railway News. Products and their quality were favourably described. The November report describes how, *'On a recent visit to Leeds, opportunity was taken to visit Ellemsee and renew our acquaintance with Mr. Potter the genial (sic) owner, who wishes to thank all his customers for understanding the delay in completing their orders* (for the Tiger motor). *This was owing, to the failure of another firm in supplying the vital parts. This delay will be only temporary'.*

The announcement was concluded with a promise of a re-release of 'Nettle' in January, and some private owner wagons in time for Christmas. Nettle appears to have been offered with a Triang motor unit and the private owners were advertised in March 1967 'on a Triang chassis'. Despite support from MRN editorials and these other belated efforts, orders continued to fall and losses mounted up. June 1967 saw the final advertisement in MRN. In August 1965 Potter had called for a twelve month moratorium on his corporate debt. He managed to survive several winding-up petitions by paying off the specific creditors, but he could not postpone the inevitable.

The winding-up order when it came on May 30th 1967, was made against John B. Potter Ltd, rather than LMC or Ellemsee, although the consequences for the model side of the business were the same. Faced with the falling model railway market Potter had attempted to diversify into other light engineering products, 'Pro-pel-aire' ventilation equipment and 'Safeti Kit' electrical wiring kits were two of these. The Receiver was damning in his listing of Potter's incompetence in his lack of understanding of the business he had ventured into, his failure to control staff and overheads and allowing his company to continue trading long after it was insolvent. Unsecured creditors were owed a total of over £16,000, Assets were valued at a bare £3000, a deficiency of £13,000 which, we may be sure, the clearance sales of LMC odds and ends, even at the most optimistic prices, would have come nowhere near covering!

Quite probably there was never a time in its whole 55 years that the Leeds Model Company was spectacularly profitable, indeed it is more likely that for many years earnings were only just above subsistence for those involved. This inglorious end was not however 'the end'. The models themselves surviving and in good health today, whether of early Leeds Model Co, R.F. Stedman & Co. or Ellemsee parentage, continue to speak both for the skills and perseverance of the founder and his hard working associates and successors.

Eames of Reading claimed in 1968 to have *purchased the entire stock in trade of Ellemsee Accessories'*, but there were more than a few companies and individuals ready to pick bare the bones and make good use of the items acquired essentially for a knockdown price. Ken Haynes wrote in 1988 to say he was one of these, but added, *'Much of the LMC stuff ended up in a shop in Leeds called the King Charles Sports and Railway Centre*, run by a man who bought cameras and golf clubs in winter to sell in the summer, and surplus railway equipment he bought in the summer to sell in the winter'*. He was obviously more successful at the latter and *'eventually scrapped the sports side and concentrated on model railways'*.

*subsequently bought by Beatties'

23   Seven Years On

Several unconnected events had conspired to initiate and stimulate the author's interest in LMC products. I had never heard of the Leeds Model Co when, in 1974, I was offered a complete layout of Leeds track, with one locomotive, the LMS Ex L&Y 2-4-2T, two LMS litho coaches and two private owner wagons, Brentnall & Cleland and J.R.Wood & Co. These had been purchased in 1936, but had been little used, the son for whom they were intended tragically dying at a young age. His grieving mother forbade her husband to dispose of any of the boy's possessions, his room being kept as a shrine to his memory. It was not until her passing in 1973, that her husband could at last dispose of the son's effects. He would take no payment for all that he handed over, but insisted that I should not sell the items and so in a way the concept of a Trust was born. Very soon after this a local model shop had an 0-4-0 saddle tank for sale, so modestly priced I could not resist it, only to find on examination that it, too, was LMC! At the time I was frequently working in Sheffield. I was not afraid to talk about my new interest in the Leeds Model Co, and as a result soon found myself in possession of a Pickersgill 0-6-0 loco, given to me by a kindly steel mill owner. I began to visit Eames at Reading, who still had a large inventory of LMC spare parts, and to look out for more LMC items, advertising my interest within the ranks of the Gauge '0' Guild, (I was at the time assistant editor of the Gazette). This brought forward 'Butler Henderson' and 'City of London' from John Hart's Midland & Southern Counties Joint Railway, a profusion of wagons, more coaches and, most importantly, an introduction to Adrian Stedman, Rex's son.

Adrian was a keen modeller and model railway operator in his own right. He had, in addition to drawings, photographs and notes, a mass of his father's leftover spare parts from his railway modelling days, as well as more recently acquired LMC spares from the time of the liquidation. Adrian took pride in working on restorations of his father's products, yet was saddened that these received very little attention and that the LMC, created by his father, was all but unknown to many model railway enthusiasts of the day. For me, the pen has always been mightier than the screwdriver and I needed little encouragement to sit down with Adrian and write 'In the Stedman Style'. This first article was to be published in Model Railway Constructor at the time of the 25th Anniversary of the Gauge '0' Guild. A second article again titled 'In the Stedman Style' was published in the MRC in May 1984, but sadly Adrian did not live to see this. He was tragically killed in a road accident the year before, shortly after completing the final draft. Joan Stedman, Adrian's widow, accepting that his work of encouraging and supporting Leeds /Stedman enthusiasts should continue, was agreeable to the establishment of the Leeds Stedman Trust, which has actively pursued those objectives. Sadly, Joan passed away in 2009. The Trust is custodian of the company records previously held by Adrian, which have been added to over the years by generous friends. The archive collection of models includes most of the locomotives and all of the standard items of rolling stock, litho and Bakelite. A smaller collection is held by the Leeds Industrial Museum at Armley Mills, Leeds. The Museum initially undertook to preserve and display the models and took possession of most of the models in Adrian's collection. When, however, the undertaking to display was withdrawn, the decision was taken to build an archive independently under direct control of the Trust. In this way models would be accessible to enthusiasts and could be taken to display or run at model railway shows. The enclosed DVD features the collection of models held by the Trust in September 2010, all of which are in full running order.

Response to the 'In the Stedman Style' articles brought forth much helpful information often from elderly correspondents, who at some stage had known Rex Stedman and others in the company. These notes have been most helpful in compiling this account. Even more contacts were made following announcement of the establishment of the Trust and publication of the 'Leeds Lines' articles in the Gauge '0' Guild Gazette. Disposing of Adrian Stedman's diffuse collection was a major task. Deciding what should be retained for the archive, what would be needed for future renovations and repairs, and what could be sold and selling it, took many months and many large tables at several Guild shows. What emerged from this was the realisation that future demands were likely to extend well beyond the limits of Adrian's stock of LMC spare parts. Thus the decision was taken to replicate those regularly in demand and make their supply an ongoing part of Trust activity. This has involved white metal and pewter casting, laser cutting of brass and tinplate, jig boring and a host of other machining operations to produce parts as simple as the Non-Lok buffers, or as complex as the front bearing and brush housing for the Series II mechanisms.

Generous assistance in the early days came from modellers who had 'unwanted stock' of LMC parts and were pleased to pass them to the Trust. A tea chest full of lithographs came from a model shop in Wellington (Salop). Most spectacularly a suitcase loaded with white metal castings was brought by Charles Curtis, from South Africa, whose father had been the LMC agent in Cape Town!

24   And now the Centenary! 2012

Proverbially of life, "The first 100 years are the worst". For any company starting just before the outbreak of the Great War, struggling through its aftermath and the years of the depression, only to be battered by World War II, survival of the first 50 years would have seemed to be a near miracle. Yet the LMC did survive those fifty years, probably at times only just, but in its 55th year it finally collapsed and died.

Does a company ever 'die' while its name and its products survive? I think not and, if a confirmation of this is required, we have only to turn to any one of thousands of cherished antiquities, widely known, lovingly preserved and aggressively sought after. Model railways do not of course date back as far as books, furniture, pottery, glassware and other artefacts of the past, yet there is no reason to suppose that they in turn, being widely known, lovingly preserved, and aggressively sought after as they are so often today, will not also be around to excite viewers of 'The Antiques Road Show' and the like in the future.

The products which have been described in the foregoing chapters and the following appendices are however worthy of a better future than being held in a bank vault, stacked up in boxes or standing on a shelf or in a glass case. They are, after all, working models and may confidently be treated as such. Of course, as modelling standards advance, as fine scale track and wheels become the norm on layouts, as electric motors and DCC technology mature, the older models may appear 'outdated', 'coarse', or 'clumsy'. These and other unflattering epithets are sometimes used by those who fail entirely to recognise or acknowledge the essential role early companies such as the LMC played in the development of model railways; a hobby for some, an all-consuming lifetime interest for others.

Looking back, it is not difficult to understand the conflicting challenges which faced Rex Stedman and his peers, who strove to develop the first 'scale' model railways. Aiming for success somewhere between tinplate 'toys' and professionally built 'one-offs', Rex took the economy in materials and production methods of the one and the realism of the other. The results achieved have been, I hope, amply illustrated both in this book and the accompanying DVD. Where did Stedman acquire such skills as a model builder, such vision as an innovator, such perseverance as an engineer? Are we born with such talents? Are we blessed with parents who inspire and support us in the directions we seem to favour; in our youth do we find a mentor able and willing to instruct and guide us? It is tempting to think that the past was more favoured than today, particularly in the field of model engineering, with individuals who have benefitted from one or all of these arguably essential components to growth and achievement.

So, as the Trust on behalf of the Leeds Model Company marks its 100th birthday, what of the future? Hopefully, the publication of this book will both extend and increase knowledge of the company and its products. Hopefully too, existing LMC enthusiasts will be further encouraged to seek out additions to their collections and effect restoration where required.

Marcus Peacock with the Trust display at the Bromley Tappers Leeds Day June 2010.

Perhaps those who have never known of the LMC will be inspired to become collectors and users of its products. In this way the locomotives, coaches wagons and all the other items and ephemera which have survived the first hundred years, will continue to be available to future generations of enthusiasts. Perhaps a slight modification to make the old 'Leeds Models Continued' slogan into 'Leeds Models Continuing' would be appropriate. No finer tribute could be given to Rex Stedman and his co-workers in the Leeds Model Company, in return for the rich legacy they have left to us.

LEEDS MODELS CONTINUING

INDEX OF APPENDICES

'Leeds – Leads'. This small yet informative leaflet was issued in 1950/51. The company announcing itself rather boldly, if somewhat unrealistically, as *probably the manufacturers of the largest range of Model Railway Equipment in the world'* asked 'Why stick to 0 gauge?' Answering the question with:

Because we are concerned with profits.
Profits come from sales.
Sales come from satisfied customers.

Gauge 0 was not surprisingly heavily promoted for 'Range, Realism and Reliability'. Critical of anything that was not 0 gauge or Leeds and objectively scornful of the 'inferior products' of competitors, the leaflet covered in brief report details of locomotives, the smoke apparatus, electrical mechanisms, track, rolling stock, power units and controllers and boxed (goods) sets.

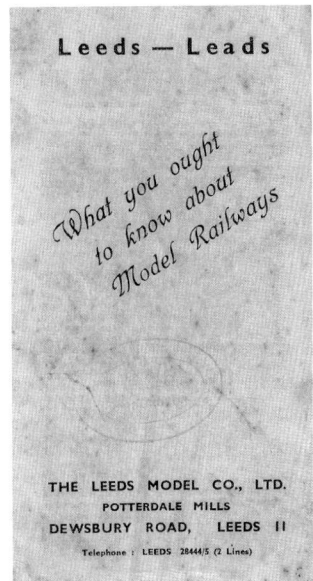

Leeds — Leads

What you ought to know about Model Railways

THE LEEDS MODEL CO., LTD.
POTTERDALE MILLS
DEWSBURY ROAD, LEEDS 11
Telephone : LEEDS 28444/5 (2 Lines)

Appendix A CATALOGUES

The first 'Preliminary' List, published in 1915, was a very modest four page affair inside paper covers. Despite Stedman's extravagant cover design for a 1916 catalogue, shown here, economy and war-time restrictions obviously intervened and illustrated covers (single colour) were delayed until 1921. As with other suppliers, LMC used the catalogue both to illustrate its products and to encourage development of railway modelling. As the company grew in size and influence, ready to run locomotives and stock were supplemented with kits and raw materials along with an increasing range of the necessary accessories, tools and drawings. Listing of agents was included, consistent with the company's post war sales policy from 1946 until 1953.

Catalogues were dated up to 1929, and thereafter from 1946. Dating of the issues from 1932 – 1939 is a matter of inspection combined with releases advertised principally in Model Railway News. Fortunately these undated issues can easily be distinguished by cover design and from 1936 by colour of the covers.

The list over details all of the original copies of catalogues currently held by the Trust. With the exception of years 1946 – 1950 which are 180mm x 250mm in landscape format, all other catalogues are in portrait layout, and are roughly of the same nominal size, approximating to A5, (148mm x 210mm).

Date	Description	Pages
May 1915	Pale blue or yellow green paper cover	4
Dec 1919	4-4-0 loco flyer with single printed sheet of revised prices	2 +1
Jan 1920	Beige	20
Mid 1920	Dark Green	20
Dec 1920	Light Brown	20
Early1921	Pale Grey, (Harewood St)	30
Mid 1921	Pale Grey,(Harewood St), overprinted Balm Road Mills	42
Late 1921	Pale Grey, Balm Road Mills	42
1922-3	Pale Green	88
1924	Cream	88
1925	Purple, Identified as 'A' and as Ist edition	114
1926 - 7	Purple, Identified as 'A' and as 2nd edition*	116
1929	Light purple 'R.F. Stedman & Co Ltd'	116
1932	Green 'Leeds Models Continued'	118
1935	Green/Cream vertical stripe	64
1936	Light and dark green with loco and dividers	64
1937	Beige and brown with loco and dividers	68
1938/9	Pink and green with loco and dividers	68
1946	Layout in brown on white**	16
1947	Loco in blue on white	16
1948	Loco in black on white	28
1949	Loco in black on white	28
1950	Loco in black on white	28
April 1952	Dark Green	92
Jan 1953	Dark Green	92
June1953	Dark Green	92
1957	Green, not illustrated	16
1959	Orange, not illustrated printed on back	17
1964	Blue, A4, paper 'Roneo' printed one side	10
1965	As 1964	10
Sept 1966	As 1964	9
1967	As 1964 but with interleaved photocopied illustrations	12

* There may also have been a first edition in 26/7, but the copy listed here appears to be the 2nd edition of the 1925 catalogue

**The layout which appears on the cover of the 1946 catalogue is that of the Whiting family's 'Hargreaves Colliery', see Chapter 8, page 28

Appendix B MECHANISMS

Mechanisms and drives provided by LMC developed progressively from the first clockwork unit issued in 1919 to the 'Tiger' motor, an upgrade of the standard 12 volt unit, which was promised in late 1965.

From the outset mechanisms were sold as separate items for scratch builders, or for fitting into other proprietary models. For this reason catalogues contained detailed drawings of the mechanism sizes with details of the materials of manufacture.

The clockwork motor illustrated had steel frames, steel and brass gears. Brake and reverse controls could be operated from the track. Speed was governed by an elegant system of calliper mounted lead weights, which against the pressure of a spring, drew a rubbing plate against a small friction pad. Even today the motors which have survived can demonstrate high performance, pulling quite heavy trains at moderate speeds for considerable distances.

Reference has been made (see Chapter 4) to the complexity of the first 8 volt electric motor introduced in 1925. Although improvements such as to the magnet,

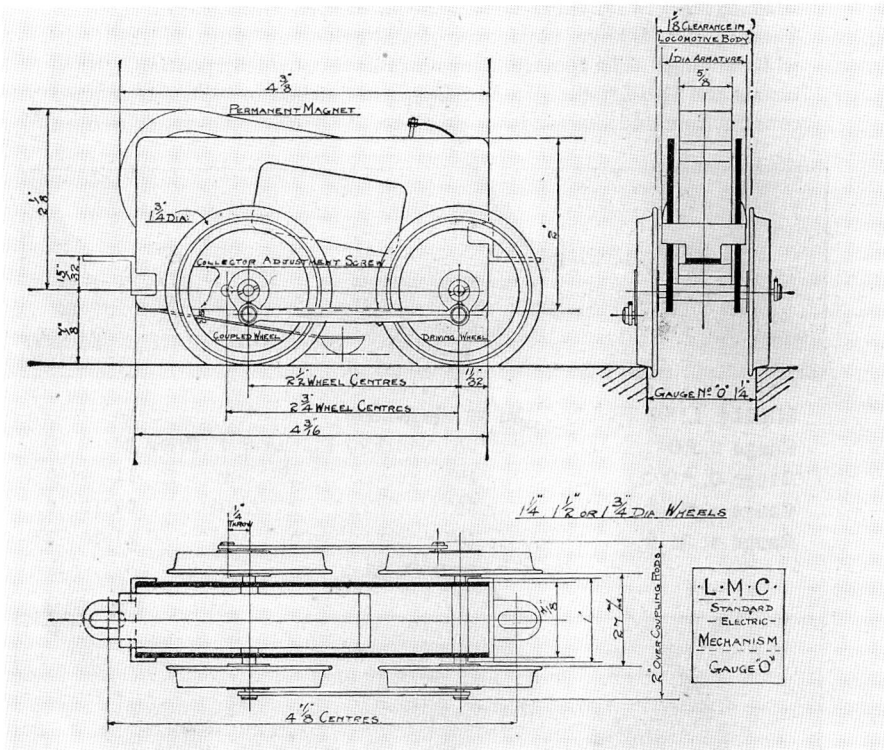

PERMANENT MAGNET

COLLECTOR ADJUSTMENT SCREW

COUPLED WHEEL DRIVING WHEEL

2½ WHEEL CENTRES

2¾ WHEEL CENTRES

4⅝

⅛ CLEARANCE IN LOCOMOTIVE BODY

1 DIA ARMATURE

GAUGE N° '0' 1¼

¼", 1½" or 1¾ DIA WHEELS

·L·M·C·
STANDARD
– ELECTRIC –
MECHANISM
GAUGE 'O'

4⅛ CENTRES

which was up-rated using Cobalt Steel and the replacement of press-formed sheet metal pole pieces with machined parts, the layout was fundamentally unchanged throughout the life of the unit.

One feature illustrated above is the single button current collector. Tender locos would normally have had a second collector fitted to the tender. Tank locos were fitted with double button collectors which were standard on later mechanisms. Outside third collectors were also available.

The introduction in 1935 of the low profile electric mechanisms for the second series of standard tanks, considerably simplified motor construction. It is clear from a study of models sold in the period from 1930 to 1935 that development was progressive. For example, the Trust's model of 'Caerphilly Castle' dated to around 1930 has the 1920s pattern brass frames, but motor and gears of the 1935 series for which the gearing ratio was stated to be 15 to 1.

The principal innovation in the new units (as well as their principal shortcoming) was the use of Newalloy (see Chapter 13) for the frames, end blocks and the casting which housed the front bearing and the brushes. These motors were supplied initially for operation at 6 to 8 volts D.C. or 20 volts A.C.

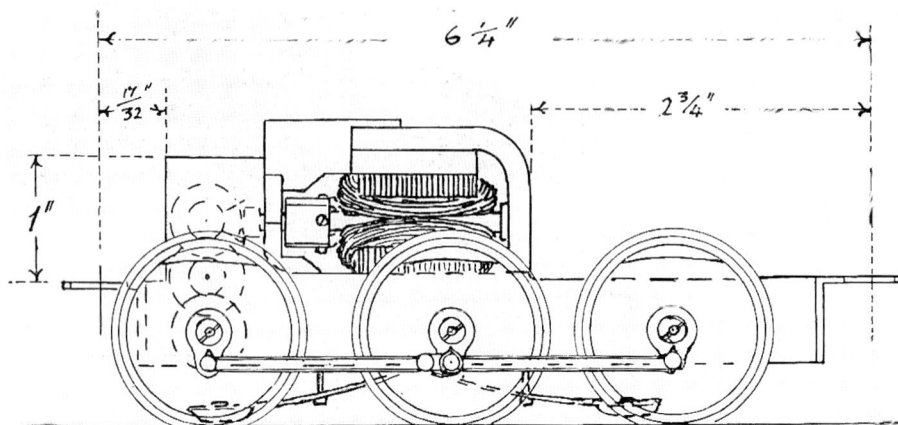

From 1946 only D.C motors were available and wired for 12 volts. The gearing was stated to be 15½ to one, which by 1948 was advertised as 13½ to 1. Inspection of the gear sets shows the change to be additional teeth to the motor shaft pinion and bevel gear on the upper lay shaft. *Care must thus be taken when restoring or repairing motor units to match these two gears.* In June 1951 the standard horseshoe bar magnet was replaced with a permanent magnet. This had a central hole to allow passage of the motor shaft and was held between rectangular steel pole pieces by a Newalloy backplate which carried the rear shaft bearing. This was certainly a more powerful motor than before but many units were again let down by the performance of the Newalloy, the backplate in particular being insufficiently robust to tolerate any swelling or distortion.

The new 'Tiger' motor promised in 1966 was dimensionally identical to its predecessor, but had four major performance enhancing refinements:

A new Alcomax III magnet
A larger diameter copper/silver commutator
Larger shaft bearings
Longer armature shaft, allowing for a flywheel to be fitted.

No record exists to show how many, if any, of these motors were produced. Advertised in May, plagiarising the Esso slogan of 'Put a Tiger in your tank' the motor was later offered in October with 'six weeks delivery'. Six months might have been a closer estimate!

An undated list for early 1967 states *'Delays have also be-devilled our new motor but we are beginning to catch up with this. Certainly worth waiting for in any event'*. (See also page 71). Frederick Rush met Potter at the Easter MRC exhibition in 1967. He reported that Potter *'was banking on an order for a vast quantity of miniature motors to keep the company afloat'* Nothing came of this and within a couple of months the Company was in liquidation.

The motor bogie, also developed in the early 1930s to power 'Nettle' and the 'Brighton Belle' (see Chapter 15), was initially set for 6 to 8 volt operation, which was changed to 12 volt after 1946. The first version of the power bogie used standard white metal coach axleguards mounted on formed brass side frames. The second version used Newalloy pressure die cast bogie sides manufactured for the Bakelite coach range. On the first version, shown here, the brushes were mounted on sprung phosphor bronze strips. For the second version the brushes were carried in moulded Bakelite housings. A single pickup button was mounted on a short insulator block and connected to the lower brush. This arrangement is less than ideal for continuous current collection and some operators have added a second collector to the trailing bogie or fitted a skate below the centre section of the vehicle body. The principal weakness of the bogie is the mounting of the motor shaft in two journals on the bogie stretchers at each end of the unit. Maintaining the alignment of these is critical to ensure correct location of the armature between the magnet pole pieces and thus smooth operation of the motor.

More powerful motors were required for the larger locomotives and for special commissions, such as the Mansted Foundry locomotives for G.P. Keen and others (see Chapter 11). For these the company had the 'Stedman-Super' motor, wound with eight poles for 12 volts D.C. or more commonly 25 volts D.C. Any wheel base could be supplied.

OPERATION AND MAINTENANCE OF LMC ELECTRIC MOTORS

LMC electric motors fall into three principal categories:

A.   Series 1 with brass frames and horseshoe magnets
B.   Series 2 with Newalloy frames and horseshoe magnets
C.   Series 2/1 with Newalloy frames and permanent bar magnets

The following faults arise from wear and/or abuse and are rectifiable to restore the motors to full working order:

1.   Mechanical wear of brass bearings – *these may be rcplaced*
2.   Demagnetising, applies only to series 1 and 2 above, and is most common with series 2. *These magnets can be re-magnetised.*
3.   Commutator loose on motor shaft. Correct position for the slots is in line with the top dead centre of the laminations. (For the motor bogie the slots must be in line with the valley between the windings). *Reposition and set using superglue or similar.*
4.   Commutator segments worn, unevenly spaced or detached. *Replace.*
5.   Windings of uneven resistance or 'burnt out'. *Rewind to 3 to 4 ohms per segment with 33 SWG (.25mm) wire for 12volts; or, 1.5 to 1.8 ohms with 28swg (.375mm) wire for 6 to 8 volts.* (Other wire diameters may be used with appropriate adjustment to the length of wire per winding).
6.   Brushes worn or unsuitable replacements fitted. Replace with correct grade copper carbon brushes.

In many cases the problem with LMC motors proves to be over oiling. It is not necessary to oil motor commutators as the copper carbon brushes are self lubricating. If oil reaches the commutator from gears and bearings, it will form a paste with the graphite from the brushes which can enter the commutator slots causing a short circuit, and sluggish running. This oily paste can also seep into the brush housing and prevents the brushes from easy movement under pressure from the plunger spring, giving problems with smooth operation, starting, and slow running. Avoid excessive oiling of gears and bearings. Keep the commutator clean by wiping with a soft rag, but not emery or glass paper. The brush housing can be cleaned through using cotton wool 'buds' or similar, and the brushes wiped clean on absorbent paper before refitting. If new brushes do not slide freely in the carriers they may require slight reduction of thickness and width. This is best achieved by sliding one wide and one narrow face across fine emery paper. After this operation the affected corners will need to be lightly re-chamfered.

Major rebuilding, requiring replacement in the series 2 and 2/1 motors of the Newalloy front bearing block and in the case of series 2/1 motors also of the rear bearing plate, may not be economically attractive. In such cases replacement of the LMC unit with a more modern motor should be considered.

Appendix C LEEDS MODEL CO. WHEEL STANDARDS

Rex Stedman had ever been an advocate of 'finer' scale than the 'steamroller' wheels current when he entered the trade. He launched his own range of white metal wheels in March 1915. Six months later he was chastised in Models Railways and Locomotives for his departure from the 'steamroller' standards and: *'At our suggestion the LMC are making coach and wagon wheels with a slightly wider tread to accommodate standard frogs. As most 0 Gauge model railway builders have found out, strict adherence to scale in width of tyres is impossible..'.*

There is almost the savagery of caricature in Stedman's drawing reproduced here, of an open wagon in the same magazine (June 1918), in which he pointedly illustrates the disparity between 'scale' wheels and 'steamrollers', and the consequent need to increase the wagon body width to accommodate the tyre dimensions. Whilst using white metal he adhered to steamroller sizes, but with Newalloy he reduced the tyre width for wagons and coaches from 5.5 to 4.0mm and the flange depth from 2.5mm to 2.0mm. Newalloy was also used to replace cast iron for locomotive and tender wheels. Similar reductions to tyre width applied, but the flange depth was further reduced to 1.5mm, making these at the time the most realistic wheels in appearance.

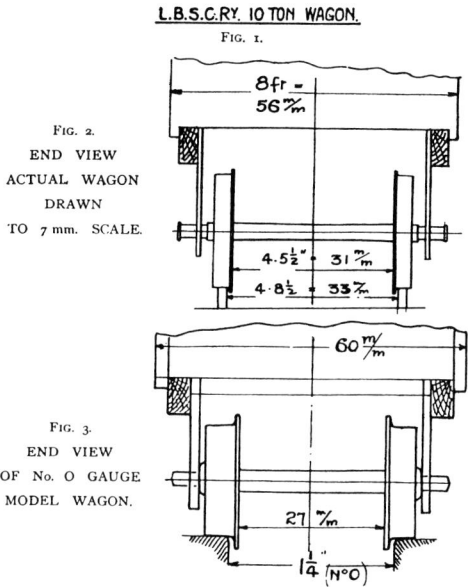

Table of tyre widths and flange depths for LMC/RFS standard wheels

Type	Material	Tyre width mm	Flange depth mm	Producer / Marks
1915 stock	White metal	5.5	2.5	LMC / LMC
1920 loco	Cast iron	5.5	2.5	LMC / Unmarked
1927 loco	Cast iron	4.0	2.0	LMC / Unmarked
1928 wagon	Zinc alloy	5.5	2.5	BING / REMOD
1929 stock	Zinc alloy	5.0	1.5	RFS / Unmarked
1930 loco	Newalloy	4.0	1.5	RFS / Unmarked
1935 stock	Newalloy	4.0	2.0	LMC / Unmarked

Appendix D SERIES I STANDARD TANK DIMENSIONS

With one exception the 'mass produced' first series of standard tanks were of identical body length, 11 inches, (279mm). The exception was the 0-4-4 model which was 10 inches long, (254mm), the one inch reduction coming off the boiler and front end of the footplate. The cab and bunker sizes were identical on every locomotive, as was the boiler diameter 1½" (38.1mm). The variations between the five models in the range were in the type of chimney, dome and safety valve, the position of splashers and footsteps forward of the cab. As noted in the main text, all models had 1½ inch (38.1mm) 16 spoke driving wheels, initially cast iron, later Newalloy and 7/8 inch (22mm) 8 spoke bogie wheels, initially white metal, later also Newalloy. Emphasis was placed on loco weights which for both clockwork and electric drive were as follows:

Wheel arrangement	Weight lbs	Weight kg	Scale weight In tons per brochure
4-4-0	2.1/4	1.02	65
4-4-2	2.1/2	1.13	73
4-6-0	2.3/4	1.25	80
0-4-4	2.1/2	1.13	72
0-6-2	2.5/8	1.19	76

Appendix E SERIES II STANDARD TANK DIMENSIONS AND VARIATIONS

As noted in the main text, the second series of standard tanks also came from one set of tooling. These locomotives all had a single standard width, boiler diameter (1¼", 31.75mm), cab height and profile. Each differed as seen below in body length and fittings. All LMC loco fittings, including those for the series I standard tanks are shown over.

Wheels	0-4-4	2-4-2	0-6-2	0-6-0	0-6-2	2-4-2	0-4-4
Company	LNER	LNER	LNER	All	LMS	LMS	SR
Origin	G.E.	G.E.	G.C.	-	L&Y	L&Y	LSWR
Length	7.7/8"	8.1/2"	8.7/8"	7.1/2"	8.1/8"	9.3/8"	8.1/8"
Wheel dia.	1.3/8"	1.3/8"	1.3/8"	1.1/4"	1.3/8"	1.1/2"	1.1/2"
Centres	2"	2"	2 x 2.5/16"	1.13/16 x 1.13/16"	2"x 2"	2.5/16"	2"
Chimney	LF/105	LF/105	LF/104	various	LF/104	LF/104	LF/105
Dome	LF/119	LF/119	LF/120	various	LF/120	LF/120	LF/119
Safety V.	LF/129	LF/129	LF/128	various	LF/129	LF/128	LF/130
Belpaire	No	No	Yes	No	No	Yes	No
Ref N°.	10	11	12	15	20	21	22
Cat N°	8120	7102	5773	various	6530	6720	126

Notes on the table: The range of locomotive chimneys, domes and safety valves at its greatest extent is shown below.

Ref No. Is the Leeds model number in the catalogue. Up to 1939, models were available with AC or DC motors and were thus listed for example LA10 or LD10. Only DC motors were offered from 1946. Models were then listed LDxx as before. Bodies only were sold, identified as L/10/B etc.

Cat No These are the numbers each locomotive bore in the catalogue depiction. Variations either side of these numbers were normal, as also were customised numbers. The 0-6-0 had numbers varying with the company, e.g. LNER 8305; LMS 8410; SR 260.

Chimneys
100 LMS Royal Scot
101 SR King Arthur
102 LNER Pacific
103 GWR King
104 Ex GC & L&Y
105 Ex GC & LSWR
106 NER
107 MR
108 CR
109 LNWR
110 GC
111 GW
112 LSWR
113 Saddle Tank

Domes
114 GC
115 LSWR
116 Saddle tank
117 CR
118 LNWR
119 GE
120 Ex CG,L&Y,LSW
121 NE
122 SR King Arthur
123 LNER Pacific
124 LMS Royal Scot

Safety valves
125 CR
126 NE
127 GC
128 Saddle tank
129 Ross pop (flat or
      curved base)
130 LSWR
131 GWR

Chimneys, Domes, and Safety Valves

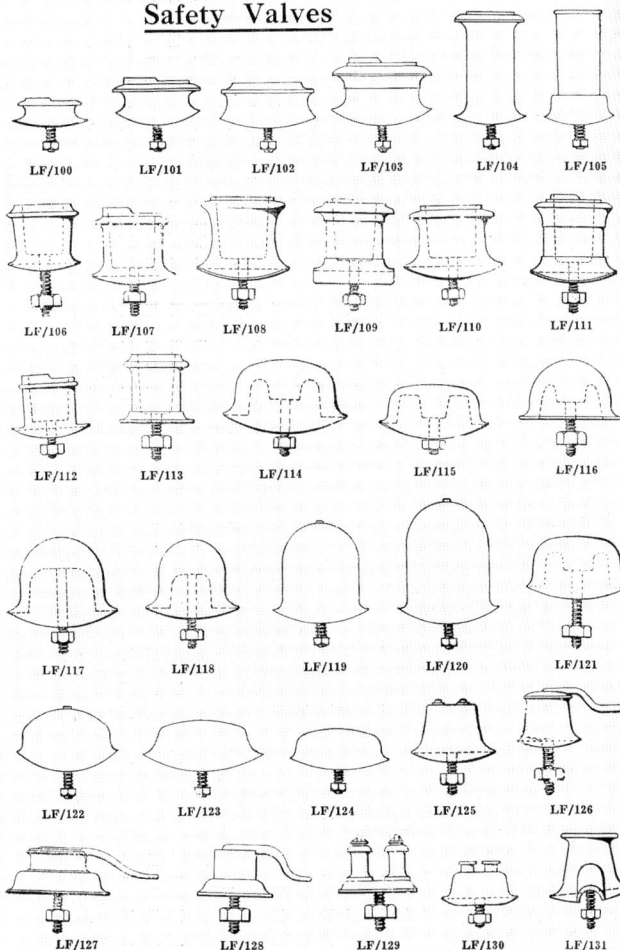

LF/100 LF/101 LF/102 LF/103 LF/104 LF/105

LF/106 LF/107 LF/108 LF/109 LF/110 LF/111

LF/112 LF/113 LF/114 LF/115 LF/116

LF/117 LF/118 LF/119 LF/120 LF/121

LF/122 LF/123 LF/124 LF/125 LF/126

LF/127 LF/128 LF/129 LF/130 LF/131

Page 38

Appendix F LITHOGRAPHS

Number W/O	Livery	Colour	Running No.	DVD
	PRE-GROUPING OPEN WAGONS			
50	NE	Light grey	V363	47
51	LNWR	Grey-green	8004	48
52	MR	Light grey	12709	48
53	GC	Blue-grey	8124	47
54	GN	Bauxite	33225	47
55	GW	Blue-grey	12509	49
	POST-GROUPING OPEN WAGONS			
56	SR	Brown	12340	50
57	NE	Black	36503	53
58	GWR	Dark brown	109458	51
59	LMS	Very light grey	304719	52
253	LMS 30T coal	Light Grey	13768	56
254	NE 50T brick	Red oxide	51001	54
	PRIVATE OWNER WAGONS			
60	R.F. Stedman &Co. Ltd	Green	30	59
61	Wood & Co	Orange	300	59
62	Brentnall & Cleland	Black	684	59
63	Warrens	Brown	1603	60
64	Coote & Warren	Brown	2176	60
65	Manchester Collieries	Maroon	12001	61
66	Cawoods	Black	1499	62
67	Michael Whitaker	Red	100	61
	BOX VANS			
170	GW pre-grouping	Blue-grey	1408	49
170	LMS	Light grey	260723	52
171	GWR	Dark green	114294	51
172	LNER	Dark green	140092	53
173	SR	Brown	44556	50
250	GW Siphon G	Brown	1278	57
251	GW Monster	Brown	591	58
252	LNER High Capacity	Grey	102497	55
	CATTLE VANS			
174	NE	Light Brown	150882	53
175	SR	Brown	764	50
176	GW	Dark green	106324	51
177	LMS	Light grey	107877	52

BRAKE VANS PRE-GROUPING

200	NE	Bauxite	71911	63
201	LNWR	Grey	382	65
202	MR	Light grey	M946	64

BRAKE VANS POST-GROUPING

200	LMS	Light grey	917	67
201	GWR	Grey	17954	66
202	NE	Bauxite	71911	63
203	SR	Brown	55975	67

COACHES

Number CO/	Livery	Colour	Running Number	
106	NE coach	Scarlet	840	19
107	NE Full Brake	Scarlet	106	20
120	LNW Composite	Brown / cream	2307	21
121	LNW Full Brake	Brown / cream	5410	22
136	MR Composite	Red	578	17
136	as LMS	Red overprinted	578	23
137	MR Full Brake	Red	159	18
137	as LMS	Red overprinted	159	24
135	LMS Brake compo	Red	358	25
150	LNER twin	Teak	6021N	26
	articulated set	Teak	6023N	26
152	LNER triple	Teak	6021N	26
	articulated	Teak	6022N	26
	set	Teak	6023N	26
138	GW Corr coach	Chocolate / cream panelled	3275	33
139	GW Corr brake	Chocolate / cream panelled	6927	34
140	GW Sub coach	Chocolate / cream panelled	3275	31
141	GW Sub brake	Chocolate / cream panelled	6927	32
142	SR Corr coach	Green	4526	29
143	SR Corr brake	Green	2127	30
144	SR Sub coach	Green	4526	27
145	SR Sub brake	Green	2127	28
106	LNER Corr coach	Teak	2253	45
107	LNER Corr brake	Teak	3627	46
108	LNER Sub coach	Teak	38295	43
109	LNER Sub brake	Teak	38364	44
134	LMS Corr coach	Crimson lake	18572	41
135	LMS Corr brake	Crimson lake	18503	42
136	LMS Sub coach	Crimson lake	3395	39
137	LMS Sub brake	Crimson lake	15478	40
138	GW Corr coach	Chocolate / cream button	3275	37

139	GW Corr brake	Chocolate / cream button	6927	38
140	GW Sub Coach	Chocolate / cream button	3275	35
141	GW Sub brake	Chocolate / cream button	6927	36

NOTE – in the above table Corr = corridor stock; sub = suburban stock

STEAM RAIL CAR

| SC1 | LNER Nettle | Green and Cream | 233 | 68 |

PULLMAN SET

Number CD/			
154	Driver	Brown and Cream, gold lining	89
155	Driver	Brown and Cream, gold lining	88
156	1st Class coach	Brown and Cream, gold lining	Hazel
157	1st Class coach	Brown and Cream, gold lining	Doris
158	3rd Class coach	Brown and Cream, gold lining	86
159	Driver	Brown and Cream, gold lining	No number
160	1st Class coach	Brown and Cream, gold lining	No name
161	3rd Class coach	Brown and Cream, gold lining	No number

Attachment of LMC litho papers

Early papers were attached using a separately applied adhesive, later papers (from mid 1930s) had a water soluble gum backing. The latter, kept in bundles, are frequently stuck together and may be parted by soaking in water. If already separated there is no need to remove the gum before the following procedure which has been found completely satisfactory for attachment of either type to timber bodies, and for photocopied papers.

The vehicle body to be clad should be stripped by soaking or scraping or coarse abrasion to remove old papers, then rubbed down with fine sandpaper to remove any raised grain, nibs or splinters. Protruding pin heads must be tapped down. Colour the corners of the body to match the litho. Colour the white cut edges of photocopied lithos to match the face colour (felt pens are good for this). Apply a smooth even coating of adhesive to one surface of the vehicle body (glue sticks are good for this), making sure the entire area is covered, then apply another smooth coat of adhesive to the litho to be attached. Line up the litho on the model and smooth out gently from the centre to the ends. It may be necessary to stretch the litho very slightly to match the length of the vehicle body and this can be done by continuing the smoothing process. When completed the litho should be in place, flat and smooth all over. Any adhesive on the surface should be carefully removed with a damp tissue. Allow the model to stand for two hours or so before tackling the other side and so on. Varnishing or other surface treatment may be applied to finish the model. Particular care should be taken with photocopied lithos. A cautious approach is recommended, testing the varnish on an end or on a corner to check that the colour is not affected.

Appendix G TYPE B SCALE MODEL GOODS ROLLING STOCK

The Trust archive regrettably does not contain an example of every item in the Type B goods vehicle range. Those vehicles which are in the archive may be seen on the DVD as below.

DVD picture	Model
66	Four wheel brake vans
69	Open wagons
69	GWR shunters truck
70	Box vans and cattle vans
71	NE High capacity box van
72	LMS Bogie open coal wagon
73	GW Siphon G
74	LNWR Single bolster wagons
75	LMS Bogie bolster wagon
76	Tank wagon
76	Tar wagon

Other models in the range are pictured below and on the following pages. The remaining item in the range is the GW Siphon H not featured but similar to Siphon G but with end doors rather than corridor connections. This model was not shown in any catalogue.

Six wheel Brake Vans

Stores dept. Drop side wagon

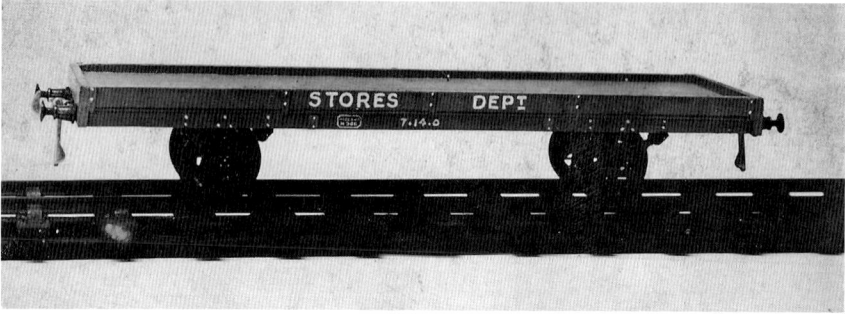

Ballast wagon

LNER tube wagon

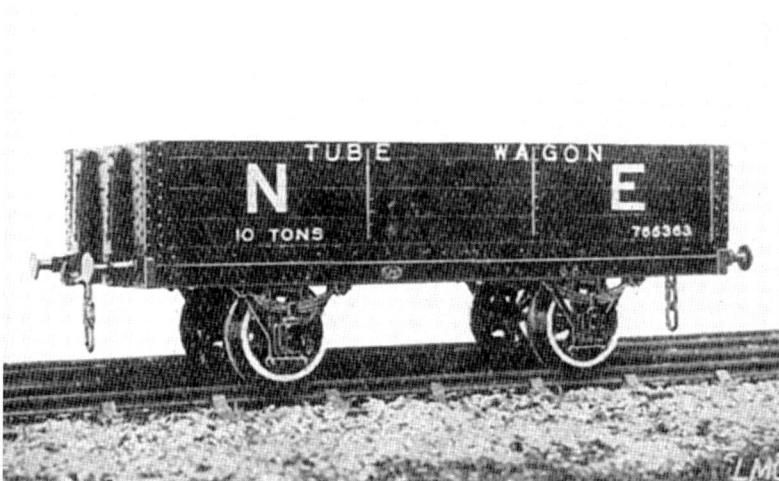

NE Horse box

GW Horse box

Appendix H AUTOMATIC AND OTHER COUPLINGS

A system of automatic coupling and un-coupling was introduced by the LMC in 1926. This was used on vehicles worked on the Wembley layout, (see Chapter 18), and on the Hordern layout exported to Australia (see Chapter 12). The couplings were short lived and were not included in catalogues after 1929. Details are best given by reference to the appropriate section of the catalogue which is reproduced below.

AUTOMATIC COUPLINGS.
GAUGE 0.

IN response to a large number of requests we are listing Sets of Parts for the Automatic Coupling which we use with such success on our Electrically Controlled Model Railways, the illustration showing clearly the method of fitting to vehicles. The ends of the coupling loop marked A must be adjusted so that they rest against the buffer beam, giving the loop the correct angle to meet and then run up the slope on the hook and so couple ; if both thin spring wires are left on, uncoupling ramps may be fitted on either side of the track.

Locomotives should be provided with the special hook at each end.

Each set contains a hook, spring, split pin, loop with brackets and screws for fixing.

AO/34   **Per set** ..   ..   .. **3/-.** Postage 1½d.

Ramps are not included but may be made from 20 S.W.G. tinplate or brass strips $\frac{3}{16}$" wide. See page 98).

The reference in the description to page 98 directs the reader to the section of the catalogue dealing with raw materials.

From the earliest days, LMC offered 'scale' 3 link couplings, which were set at a size suitable for both 0 and 1 gauges. It was claimed, probably justifiably, that the hook would stand a total load of 1000 '0 gauge tons' (i.e. 27 lbs or 12kg). More significantly the chain was made to fall 1/8" (3.2mm) short of the 0 gauge rail level, so as not to foul points or the raised centre third rail of electrified systems. This chain, to the same standard size, was later produced by Gordon Usherwood of Fleet (Australia) for his own production of couplings. Stocks of this product have survived and in recent years been made available to the Trust for restoration and new-build.

The popularity of single or 'drop-link' link couplings and their particular suitability for operation with small radius curves necessitated their supply by LMC and from 1920 onwards they were a standard catalogue item. Unless specifically ordered to the contrary they were fitted to all rolling stock until 1928. Several designs in production to date closely resemble the LMC product.

The first bogies and axleguards cast in hard white metal by Stedman were for his hand built models. The pages which follow are from the 1920 catalogue and very closely depict the products. The coach and van bogies were rigid, soldered up with the wheel sets in place. The diamond frame bogie sides were attached to the bolster by screws and lock nuts. The sides were free to move independently allowing for full compensation.

Coach & Wagon Bogies.

Since we started making these bogies, they have had a tremendous sale. As will be seen from the illustrations, all details are included, and they have the effect of showing off to perfection the coach or wagon fitted with them.

The frames are Oxydized Finish, the wheels of the English type having red-brown centres and white rims. The American type, with outside equalizing bar, is much favoured by the G.W. Rly.

The wheels fitted to these are the pressed steel type and have white rims only. All bogies are complete with rubbing-plates and are all ready for screwing to the underframes.

English Pattern.

4 Wheeled.

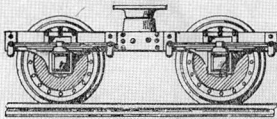

Gauge 0. L.N.W. or G.N. type
Per pair   5/4   Postage 6d.
Gauge 1.   L.N.W. type only
Per pair   7/2   Postage 6d.

6 Wheeled

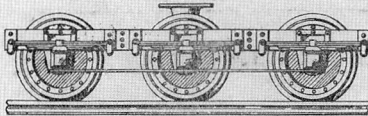

Gauge 0. L.N.W. or G.N. type. Per pair 7/6 post. 6d.
Gauge 1. L.N.W. type only
Per pair 10/6 post free.

American Type.

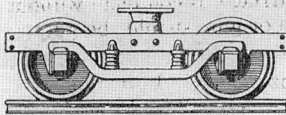

Gauge 0. Per pair   5/9
postage 6d.

Diamond Frame.

These are modelled from those used by many of the leading Railways for High Capacity Wagons, and two or three of these wagons at least should be included on every Model Railway.

Gauge 0. Per pair   5/- postage 6d.

The single axleguard patterns (shown below) continued in production into the late 1920s, and as with all LMC items were sold separately, as well as being incorporated into the Type B and C models.

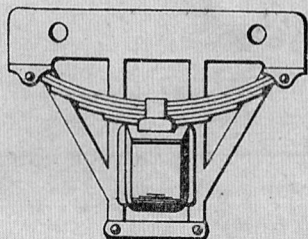

Axle Guards.
Oxydized Finish.

These are clean die castings in hard anti-friction metal. All holes are in, and they only require screwing to the sole bars. The illustrations are full size.

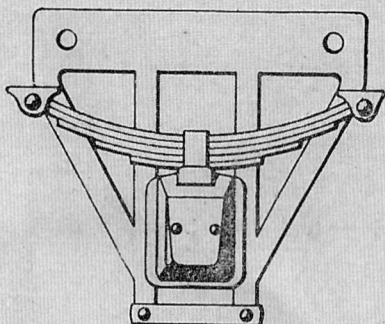

Wagon Type.

Gauge 0.   Per doz.   2/2   Postage 2d.
   „   1.   „   „   2/10   „   3d.

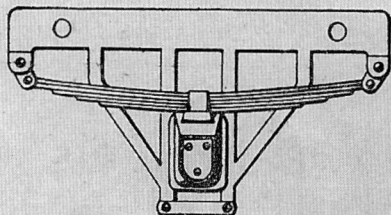

Carriage & Van Type.

These are new this season, and we are the first firm to produce them commercially. They have the correct 5ft spring and are suitable for four or six wheeled coaches and vans.

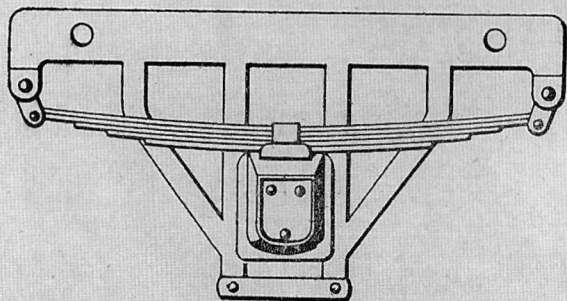

Gauge 0.   Per doz.   2/6
   „   1.   „   „   3/-
       Postage 3d

SPECIAL SCREWS for fixing the above axles guards to the sole bars. Per doz. 1d.

The hard white metal bogies were phased out progressively in favour of lower cost units designed for the Type A coaches and vans shown over. The compensated diamond frame bogies were retained but cast in the softer white metal used for all other items then in the range.

The bogie frames shown here were pressed from tinplate, and cast white metal axleguards were initially soldered into place, later cast in situ.

A similar approach was used for the goods stock. White metal dummy springs and axleboxes (bearing the letters LMC), were cast into a tinplate bolster stamped to provide the axlebox support frames.

When Rex Stedman took over LMC and ran the company under his own name he obliterated the LMC letters from the mould. The crude punch marks were later dressed to provide a slight dome on the box cover. Axleguards may thus be broadly dated from the axlebox. Pre 1928, with 'LMC'; 1928 - 1932 stamp impressed; post 1932, domed.

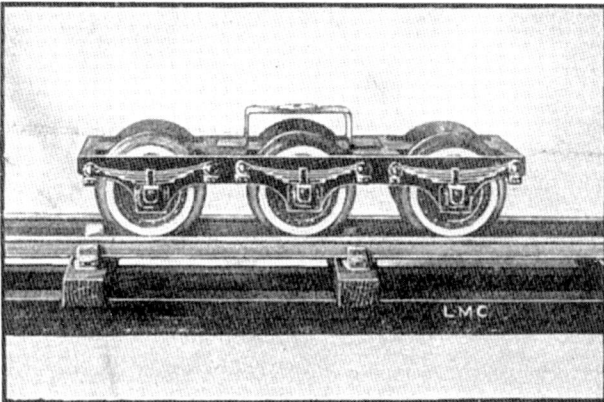

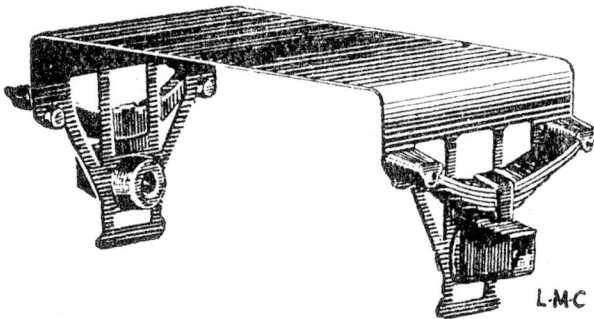

The move to pressure die casting provided the opportunity to simplify the wagon axleguards still further in that, with the higher strength metal, the full axleguard could be cast and attached to a simple bolster by peening protruding pins on the back face of the casting into holes provided on the folded edge of the tinplate strip. These bolsters were attached to the floors of wooden wagons by a pair of centrally positioned screws. The bolsters were later fitted with tabs for attachment through slots in the wagon floor to the Bakelite stock and this method was also used for wooden litho stock produced from 1935 onwards.

Pressure die cast bogies of '8 ft.' (56mm) wheelbase were produced for the Bakelite coaches. They were ready before the coaches and were thus fitted to some of the last items sold in the litho coach range. The bogies were made up from five castings; two sides, two end stretchers, and a central bolster. The sides carried a central spigot which was located in the bolster. The stretchers were attached to the sides by 9BA screws. These were not fully tightened to allow for compensation when running.

 The bogie sides were also adapted to fit the motor bogie for the Sentinel Railcar 'Nettle' and the Brighton Belle Pullman set. Fitted to the trailing bogie of Nettle and the motor cars and to the other coaches in the Brighton Belle set, these bogies made a considerable improvement in the appearance of both items.

Once again, the use of less than pure zinc in the Newalloy formulation has led to failures of some or all parts of the original bogies. Replacements cast in pewter are available from the Trust, but because of small differences in the final size of the castings, these cannot be substituted one for one with parts from original Newalloy units.

Appendix K SMOKE UNITS

Smoke units* were introduced in 1949 and were fitted to the 0-4-0 saddle tank in the train sets and sold separately or fitted as an optional extra in the saddle tanks and the freelance 4-4-0 locomotives.

The smoke was generated in a die cast box fitted in the loco cabs, (shown below in the cab of an 0-4-0ST). The box contained a heater coil wrapped in absorbent fibre. The box had inlet and outlet ports; the inlet connected to a cylinder fitted to the front of the mechanism, the outlet port was connected to the loco chimney.

The heater was connected in the circuit by a switch (seen above lifted clear of the cab but in operation set across the connecting pipes in the loco cab), under a removable roof. One wire connects the box to the loco cab backplate, the second wire connects the box to the switch. The other pole of the switch is connected to the loco pick-up. The feed point for oil is the brass bung set as can be seen at the right hand end of the smoke box. A hypodermic syringe, or similar, is recommended for filling in this inconvenient location. Occasionally when units were (repeatedly) allowed to run dry a carbonised layer of fibre would accumulate around the filament and prevent fresh oil reaching the surface of the coil. The heater wire might in the worst cases burn out

*Provisional patent 16956, May 1949.

Originally the connecting pipes were rubber tubing and over time this has perished. Replacement with modern plastic tubing (model aircraft fuel lines, etc), is recommended. The pumping cylinder was made from brass and the piston, which was driven by a cam on the front, (driven) axle of the mechanism was made from Newalloy. Inevitably, many of the pistons have swollen and seized in the cylinder. These may be removed and replaced with aluminium or steel parts, to restore the pumping function. A light application of thin oil assists movement and maintains the efficiency of the seal between piston and cylinder. The pump components are shown here:

Upper left,:
Brass cylinder with outlet pipe and bracket for attachment to upper frame of mech.

Lower left. :
Cam which push fits on the boss of the final drive gear

Lower centre:
Cam follower with connecting arm (detached) to piston .

Right:
Piston with slotted boss for connection to arm.

Writing to the Trust in 1986, the late Norman Green advised that he had been told by Rathbone that the smoke units used 'Thelson' Oil, with the addition of 5% oil of lavender to 'sweeten-up' the odour. Oil was supplied in small glass tubes sealed with a cork, and identified 'Ellemsee Smoke Reagent'. Tubes were sold for 6 pence (2½p) each and carried the warning 'No other substance must be used'

Despite this warning other modern smoking oils and even baby oils work well and certainly most of these have a less unpleasant smell!

Experience today is that the corks fitted in the original smoker oil glass tubes prove most difficult to remove without breaking the tubes. Drilling a small hole and using a syringe is recommended to empty the contents without loss.

Appendix L TRACK

Components for track making, rail, chairs, fishplates, sleepers and pins (spikes) were first offered by the LMC in 1921, under the description of 'Permanent Way'. The rail was hard brass bullhead, the chairs die cast white metal and cast relatively coarse-sized fishplates. Other than the sleepers, which were sized for each gauge, the track components were sold as 'suitable for gauges 0 and 1', as they undoubtedly were.

Within a year the company greatly expanded its offerings of track and two new standards were available :

Tinplate, the least expensive and completely suitable for clockwork operations, the most common at the time, was in effect portable 'toy–train' track. The track was manufactured, possibly by Bing, in short three sleepered lengths, 11" straights and 12¼" long 2 ft radius curves for 0 gauge (6ft radius for gauge 1). Moving frog points, acute angle crossings, single crossovers and parallel points made possible as comprehensive a layout as available elsewhere at the time. Lengths were connected with opposed pins and secured with spring catches.

Ready laid track, was supplied with the choice of sheradised (zinc coated) steel or brass rail. This used the components of the Permanent Way system, with the additional option of third rail for electric operation. For fishplates, the heavy section white metal castings were replaced by thinner and more realistic steel or brass sprung sheet pressings. With 16 sleepers to the yard in 0 gauge, this track was still some way from being of realistic appearance, but it was significantly superior to the tinplate track and still portable if required. Points, double junctions, single and scissors crossings, (complete with point levers and rodding), 45 degree, 60 degree and right angle crossings completed the range. As a guide to using the track, a selection of layout schemes was given in the 1922/3 catalogue with a guide to overall sizes and prices.

The catalogue for 1924 replicated the offerings of the previous year. The tinplate track does not appear in the 1925 list and for the first time third rail electrification gets a short paragraph. Buyers were asked to specify raised or level setting of the conductor rail. The company advised 'raised' third rail as 'being less complicated at points and crossings'.

Further changes followed in the catalogue for 1926 -7. For the first time the thin trapeziform brass conductor rail (see page 103) was shown with the special chairs and fishplates required for its installation at a height 1/8" above the running rails. This could be used either for centre or outside third installation. (Both systems were in favour at the time). Clearly an unsuccessful product, new 'Allmet' track made its one and only appearance in this issue of the catalogue. Aimed at further price reduction this, as the name suggests, was of all metal construction using unpainted heavy tinplate U-section sleepers resistance welded to the track. Curves were produced with set super elevation of 3/16"! Electric track had a brass centre rail set on insulated supports. Points were promised to be 'ready shortly'. A major problem with the track was its mismatched height with the existing ready laid track. To offset this problem the company offered additional sleepers of special thickness. With this and its rather ungainly appearance it is hardly surprising that 'Allmet' proved to lead nowhere. At the end of 1928 the buyout of LMC and formation of R.F. Stedman & Co. quickly saw the abandonment of this type of track.

Two years before this, and before the well publicised introduction by W.S. Norris of his 'fine scale' 0 gauge layout, Stedman produced a batch of parts for fine scale track. He used these to make up some demonstration sections including points and crossovers suitable for 29mm back to back wheels with narrow tyres and shallow flanges, similar to the 'fine scale' wheels of today.

Shown here with the hand held die for casting them, (one at a time!) are the tiny chairs for the fine scale track. Lower left is the wooden handle with which the mould is held and above this is the withdrawable plunger, which forms the gap for the rail. The sprung pin which ejects the finished casting can be seen in the mould. The lever on the right swings over the mould and provides the pouring hole. For comparison standard scale 0 gauge chairs are set alongside.

Made from these parts, a right hand double junction, was illustrated with an accompanying letter from Rex in the April 1927 issue of Model Railway News. Commenting on this development in a letter (1984) to the Trust, Frederick Rush, who knew Stedman well and was considering financing the company in further developments states *'I don't know of anyone who had a layout with his fine scale rail, but I'm pretty certain that he made the tools for it, and probably rolled* (the rail) *himself'*. There is no evidence to suggest that any of these finer scale parts were ever produced in quantity or sold commercially at any other time. Bought in parts would have been used for finer scale wheels if ordered to be fitted to models supplied in the 1950 – 1960 period.

Electric Third Rail. In a departure from using standard rail section for current collection, in 1927, Stedman produced small section light trapeziform rail. Described right, this rail was two thirds the price of running rail. It was used intermittently into the 1950s.

Electric Third Rail.

OWING to the increasing popularity of Electric propulsion on Model Railways, we offer a special section of rail for use as a Conductor rail, together with chairs for same. This new rail is in every way superior to the old method of using brass or copper strip or an ordinary running rail for this purpose. The chairs are designed to raise the 3rd rail ½-in. above the level of the running rails. If all level 3rd rail is required, and the track is laid on ½-in. sleepers, the chairs should be mounted direct on the baseboard, between the sleepers.

RAIL. This is drawn in hard brass to the section illustrated, and is supplied dead straight and free from kinks. When bending to a curve it should be laid on a flat surface and gently bent to the required radius by finger and thumb.

PW/20 ... ... Per 3-ft. length, **4d.**

CHAIRS. Neatly designed die-castings, a sliding fit on the rail. Holes are provided in the two lugs on the base for fixing with PW/8 spikes.

PW/21. Per gross, **6/-**; per half-gross, **3/3**; per dozen, **7d.**

FISHPLATES. Pressed from spring brass to fix snugly on the rails forming a perfect electric connection.

PW/22. Per gross, **6/-**; per half-gross, **3/3**; per dozen, **7d.**

LMC also accepted commissions to build track. Writing in MRN in September 1939, D. Clegg, owner of the Darley Bank model railway states *'Leeds Model Company made the track for me according to my specifications, without battens, laid direct onto fourteen ply-wood. The rail used is brass and not exact scale as used by Mr. Norris. Outside collector rail system is employed'*. The outside third rail appears from photographs to be standard bull head rail, rather than the lower section LMC trapeziform conductor rail. At the end of the article Mr. Clegg expresses thanks to Moore and Simpson for the advice and help given. This is all but the last mention of Moore in any connection with the LMC.

Factory made 0 gauge track with 40 sleepers per yard was offered from 1948 to 1953, with a very complicated six track layout with crossovers, scissors, diamond crossings and slips being illustrated in the 1949 and 1950 catalogues. The requirement of a single customer, this masterful work illustrated every type of point and crossing which the company would produce to special order only. Several of these superbly made set pieces survive today in full operating order.

From 1935 the 'Ready Laid' track was renamed 'Metalway', but was otherwise substantially unchanged in its format throughout the 1940s and 50s until in the early 1960s when the company ceased to supply made up track. Metalway with trapeziform conductor rail was used in the 1950s train sets.

Appendix M SIGNALS

Parts for the building of signals were from 1912 the first products made by the Leeds Model Company. Throughout his time in LMC, and up to the end with R.F. Stedman and Co, Rex paid considerable attention to this part of the product range. He regularly added items to assist railway modellers to achieve the maximum of realism in the appearance of their signals and their operation. It is arguable that nowhere in the railway world is there so much diversity as in signals. Rex's 1920 catalogue lists factory made models including, N.E. slotted post and G.N. somersault varieties. The 1924 catalogue carries illustrations of factory made single arm signals, two and three arm bracket signals and a four arm gantry, all factory made. Two standards were offered:

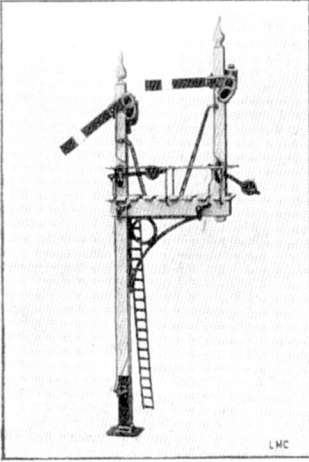

    (a)   Scale Models
    (b)   Super-Detail scale models

The Scale Models, were as their name suggests of correct scale dimensions, but as shown below carried the minimum of detail consistent with realistic appearance and effective operation.

The Super-Detail models (above left) used the same parts as the scale models but were enhanced with platforms, handrails, ladders, operating chains etc. They were typically double to three times the price of the Scale Models.

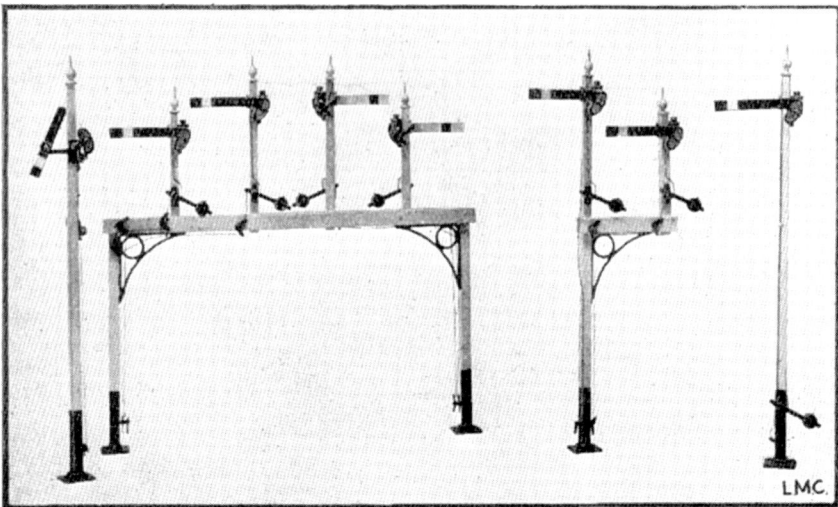

Increasing pressure on the workforce due to the explosion of the product range at that time inevitably led the company to encourage modellers wanting signals to 'do-it-yourself'. Certainly the would-be signal builder was not kept short of the necessary parts! Of the one hundred and thirty plus catalogued items in the company range at that time, just under one third were for signals.

A most impressive range of signals was built into the 1928 layout for the Hordern family in Australia (see Chapter 12). These were lit by 2 volt pea bulbs fitted into specially made lamps. The feed wires to the bulbs were hidden in a slot cut into the signal post. With electrified layouts well established, LMC also offered solenoids for signal operation, and these were fitted to the Hordern layout on which signals and points were operated from a 60 lever frame. Under R.F. Stedman & Co. the range and variety of signals, including a newly introduced working ground signal reached its peak. From 1932, full kits of parts for signal building were introduced and although the company continued to offer factory built signals, in both gauge 0 and gauge 1 the price of these was unlikely to have encouraged substantial demand in those financially straightened times.

Some of the range of individual signal parts was featured in the 1946 and 1947 catalogues, but in 1948 a single arm upper quadrant, home – as shown - or distant, signal was introduced. The models were factory made with round metal posts secured in a rectangular base and were complete in detail with spectacles, backshade, dummy lamp, ladders, weight and lever and guide pulley. They were individually boxed (see Page 114) and labelled under "Ellemsee", manufactured by the Leeds Model Co Ltd. Multi-arm models were promised for 'later development'. This promise, however, was never fulfilled.

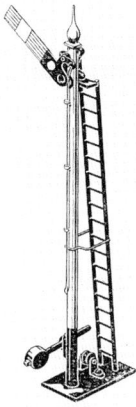

SH/7

One further signal was introduced by LMC in 1953, before the ultimate slide into liquidation began. This was appropriately called 'Dummylite' (illustrated here). It was a modest attempt at an electric signal, without any wiring required, a hand operated slide exposed green or red in the spectacles! Described as 'an ideal practical adornment' for any size of 0 gauge layout, it survived into the 1957 price list, but not thereafter. A reduced range of signal fittings and accessories appear in the 1959 price list, but not in any subsequent list. Quite a few parts were however left in stock, and were acquired by various individuals in the liquidation sales. Such lots have proved invaluable in restoring early LMC signals, or constructing replicas of the very fine Scale Models manufactured by Rex Stedman and his co-workers.

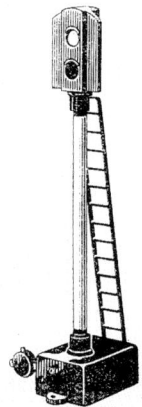

As model makers the Leeds Model Company could notionally provide for every requirement to complete the railways which was their core business and so offered a custom service for buildings. It is clear from inspection of certain items that they are unquestionably of LMC origin, but others, such as buildings – even

if they are reasonably similar to the various pictures in the catalogues – prove more difficult to identify with confidence, especially as they may have no manufacturer markings. The fullest listing of buildings appears in the LMC catalogues from 1925 to 1932 and the R.F. Stedman catalogue for 1929. These were high quality scale models and were very expensive for the time. After 1936, the sizes, and appearance changed, and the prices of the much simplified buildings were far more reasonable. The signal cabin above in 1927 was priced at

£3/3/0, (£3.15). In 1926, a 'cheaper version' of the Signal cabin was listed but not illustrated. In 1937 the price for the version shown right was 6/6, (32.5p).

Early catalogues detailed single and island platforms of two lengths; 36", (914mm) and 48", (1.22m) for 0 gauge; and 52", (1.32m) and 70" (1.78m) for Gauge 1. The range ultimately included double and single road

engine sheds; goods shed and platform (from 1936), plate layers huts, coal offices and nine various domestic buildings; rail, road and foot bridges, and single and double track tunnel mouths. The Scherzer rolling bridge first catalogued in 1922/3 was later also sold in kit form.

There were just three trackside accessories; buffer stops, a loading gauge and a water column. The early buffer stops were of basic design in wood, but a rail built unit of more realistic appearance was not introduced in the catalogue until 1935. The rail built buffer stop and the water column alone survived to be listed in the post 1945 catalogues.

A bookstall (attributed to the Model Engineer), which could be purchased assembled, as well as from 1929 as a kit, was not continued after 1932.

The set of platform furniture was introduced in 1924 and the correct and complete set is shown here, in box, with the original cover. All of the pieces were cast and painted in the factory and have the initials L.M.C. clearly embossed on their back faces. These also were discontinued from 1932.

In common with many model railway manufacturers in the early days of electrification, the LMC had no specific products to offer for layout operation. Options available to operators typically varied from full mains connection to storage batteries (accumulators). Transformers with 240v to 12v or 24v, AC and DC appeared later. LMC were offering electric drive from 1922 but it was not until 1925 that a range of accumulators was offered in the catalogue and a year later before a simple six speed reversing controller (pictured right) appeared. These units, of basic but robust construction had been proved by their extensive use at the Wembley Model Railway Exhibition in 1925. The first 'Hints on electrification' appeared in the 1931 catalogue, showing various systems of current delivery to the speed controllers, but it was not until 1936 that a range of five Shenphone DC transformers (one such pictured left) was offered alongside the same six speed single or double controllers. One year later, and at marginally lower prices, a more modern Shenphone transformer/controller, (pictured right) complete with ammeter, was offered, but these did not re-appear in the post war catalogues. In 1948 the company announced that work was in hand to develop a new power controller incorporating speed and direction switching. The same announcement also appeared in the catalogues for 1949 and 1950, but the accompanying price lists showed a range of Kirdon made transformers under the names 'Parpak', 'Parpak Contro' (this unit included speed and direction controls), 'Kirdon' and 'Weston Junior'. These units did not feature in the 1952 or 1953 catalogues but continued to be offered and listed on and off in price lists up to 1964. A smaller simplified system based on the 'Parpak Three' rectifier with a separate speed control, was available in conjunction with the train sets offered in the 1950s. These units were finished in black crinkle paint and neatly packaged in brown mock leatherette boxes matching the packaging of the train sets. The variety of motors and mechanisms supplied by LMC across the range of standard and special locomotives from the early 1920s to 1966, makes it difficult today to specify or recommend any single unit for power delivery and control.

Appendix R   DRAWINGS

As with any engineering establishment, drawings were an essential adjunct to parts manufacture, assembly and finishing. Rex Stedman had demonstrated his talent for draughtsmanship in his youth. Two such examples held in the Trust are a drawing of girder work from his 1908 examination at Battersea Polytechnic and, from the same year, his 'Eswyn Model Works' locomotive drawings (after Eswyn Road, London SW17, where he was living at the time). A further set of early but undated locomotive drawings, are labelled as from the 'Eswyn Model and Mechanical Drawing Office' (Stedman and Taylor).

The drawings of Henry Greenly served Stedman well in the first days of model building and the Greenly range of drawings continued to be offered by the company up to 1928. From what is in the archive it appears that Rex drew all of the 'specials' and the often 'one-off' super detail models. Relatively few of these pencil drawings on card were converted to blueprints. From the early 1920s there were at least two other competent draughtsmen in the company who produced drawings for blueprints of many of the standard items including rolling stock and lineside items. The LMC range of drawings continued to grow covering the series I standard tanks and other production models, but with the addition of some of the special orders, models which never featured in the catalogues. By 1929, there were sixty two LMC locomotive drawings listed in the catalogue, along with twenty-two further drawings for coaches, buildings, signals and other accessories. The locomotive drawings, in particular, provide a useful check in attempting to establish the provenance of older models which appear to be of LMC origin. Models built other than by the LMC might well include LMC parts but, if there is also a drawing, the possibility is substantially increased of the model being entirely of LMC manufacture.

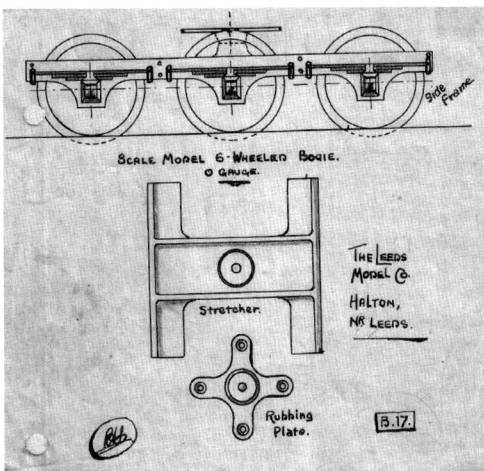

Railway Company drawings held in the archive show that there appeared to be little problem in the early 1920s obtaining details of various locomotives, and thus producing accurate scale models of them. The drawing produced by Rex in 1917, shown here, details the cast white metal bogie used on his handbuilt coaches. The painstakingly detailed and accurate work fully reflects Stedman's approach to modelling.

In the 1935 catalogue a 'new and wide' series of some two hundred drawings was listed covering locomotives and coaches of the big four. At the same time the range of LMC drawings was reduced. All of the pre-grouping locomotive drawings and company model drawings were withdrawn, leaving only locomotives of the big four and the Metropolitan Railway, thirty four drawings in all. The existing range of 'Useful Drawings for Model Engineers' for coaches, signals and trackside items (twenty four in all), was retained as were the seventeen drawings for track, points, crossovers etc.

Diane Brice, who along with her husband Phil, holds the archive of master Skinley drawings confirmed that this 'new and wide' 1935 range of drawings were indeed the work of John Skinley. The current Skinley numbering for 0 gauge places a '7' in front of the numbers used in the LMC listing, e.g. list number 241, GW 57XX 0-6-0 Pannier tank, becomes 7241. It is therefore possible to work back from the pre-war LMC listings to the current Skinley reference.

After the war, the LMC locomotive and rolling stock drawings were withdrawn from sale, leaving only the LMC track and point drawings in place. The company, in making this decision accepted that the Skinley range of over five hundred different items very effectively covered the field. John Skinley was thoroughly recommended for the accuracy of his drawings and the excellence of his service!

The promotion of kit building in 1948 required a new set of drawings to facilitate assembly and these were produced by F. Poulter. Those for which copies are held in the archive are numbered as follows:

ASS/89 and 89A 0-6-0T (second series) freelance tank locomotive
ASS/90 and 90A 2-4-2T (second series) LMS tank locomotive
ASS/91 and 91A 0-6-2T (second series) LNER tank locomotive
ASS/95 and 95A 0-4-0T inside cylinder saddle tank locomotive
ASS/100 and 100A 4-4-0 inside cylinder freelance tender locomotive
ASS/101 tender for ASS100
ASS/105 Sentinel Cammell rail car

The gaps in numbering suggest that other kits were planned, but to date no other similar drawings have come to light, nor models suggesting build other than in the LMC factory.

Appendix S TRANSFERS

Inspection of early handmade stock shows that, for the most part, hand lettering was used. The first use of transfers was for the 'mass-production' first series of standard tanks. Transfers were used both for tank and bunker panels and boiler bands. These covered the various liveries and styles of most of the pre-grouping companies. Initially in 1921, transfers were made for the North Eastern, London & North Western and Midland railways. Great Northern, Great Eastern, Caledonian, Great Central, London & South Western and London Brighton & South Coast were added in 1922. A similar range plus G.W.R. was available for the 0-4-0 tanks. The early 4-4-0 (pictured below) demonstrates this first approach to transfer lining and lettering, much of which has remarkably survived years of use. A small oval transfer, gold on black carried the letters LMC and was attached to the splashers or smokebox saddle of locomotives and the solebars of rolling stock. This distinct plate can be seen on the loco below.

Great Western livery was offered for the Series I standard tanks from 1925, but in common with the other three of the big four liveries offered at the same time, this was achieved with single letter and number transfers, with hand painted lining

where appropriate. This revised approach was first depicted with LNER, SR and LMS liveries in the catalogue for 1926/7. The scale model locomotives, 'Butler Henderson', 'Sir Sam Fay' and the like had transfers for their names as well as for lettering and numbers.

Lettering, numbers and boiler band transfers were used for the second series of standard tanks, but other lining on the tank sides and bunker were, as for the post-grouping Series I tanks, hand painted.

A new range of transfers was required for the Bakelite wagons, vans and coaches. For coaches the range included numbers 1 and 3, 'First' and 'Third' for the coach classes, 'Luggage', 'Guard' and sheets with ten pairs of different numbers, each in the style of the big four companies. The vans and wagons were supplied for by sheets of paired numbers with the initials of each company above them. The styles of these various transfers can be seen on DVD pictures 87 to 96.

Throughout the life of the company a rectangular transfer with gold lettering on black announced *'Manufactured throughout in Great Britain by the Leeds Model Co Ltd'*. This was attached to most standard locomotive models and Bakelite stock. A printed paper version of this notice was also used from time to time.

The instructions set out below were given for use of LMC varnish fix transfers. (Such LMC transfers that have survived and remain available today, being anything from 80 to 90 years old, are unlikely to provide as satisfactory a result as modern transfers of any type). *Care should be taken using these transfers; it may be a wise precaution to experiment on painted tinplate or similar before working on a finished model.*

1. Divide the backing paper from the face of the transfer by inserting a fine knife edge or similar.
2. Cover the back (glossy side) of the transfer with a thin coat of gold size or other quick drying varnish.
3. Allow the size/varnish to become tacky before placing the transfer down in the correct position.
4. Once the position is assured, press the transfer well down with a clean cloth and allow to stand for 30 mins. or more until the size/varnish is dry.
5. Soak the transfer tissue with a few drops of water until it is completely free.
6. Press down the transfer with a moist sponge, allow to dry fully.
7. A thin coat of varnish over the transfer will help prevent damage and preserve its condition.

Appendix T BOXING AND LABELLING

At no time in the existence of the Leeds Model Company was there a uniform style of boxing such as, for example, with the Hornby range. LMC labelling was erratic in style, colour and information provided. At certain times very cheap cardboard was used, remaining examples of which today are usually found taped together or in separate pieces. Small boxes, typical of the one shown here for signal parts were more robust. They usually had a printed label on the box top with details of the contents hand written alongside.

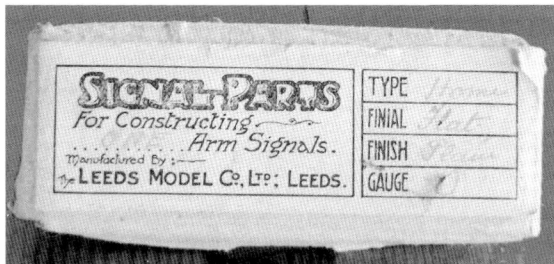

Very few boxes (a random few it would seem) had a coloured paper cover. This approach appears to have been introduced during the time the Bristol Model Company was involved with the LMC. One such box covered in green was used for the water crane.

Arguably the box for Station accessories came nearest to being a quality presentation, despite the hand drawn labelling! (see page 107).

Larger boxes for locomotives and rolling stock were plain cardboard printed on the lid as shown below.

The box content was frequently identified on one end with a handwritten description, at other times a rubber stamp was used. From the limited evidence available, it appears that Rex Stedman during the time he ran the company under his own name, (1928 – 1932), used plain boxes with rubber stamping of his company name and address on the lids and, on one end, a stamped general description of the contents, completed with handwritten particulars.

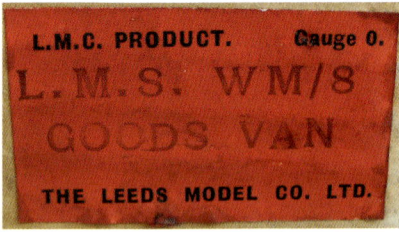

From 1932, red and green labels were used, on various designs of box. Red labels were used for ready to run models, green labels were used on boxes containing kits of parts. The contents were identified by rubber stamp or handwritten.

From 1936 standard corrugated cardboard boxes were introduced for the Bakelite stock. These boxes were typically labelled as the example shown. The

boxes had a removable inner wrapper also of corrugated board which enabled the item to be lifted from the box. Coach boxes carried a warning 'PLEASE READ BEFORE UNPACKING', with the instruction that the wrapper should be used to remove the coach from the box. It was emphasised that this method alone should be used primarily as a precaution against breaking the delicate window frets by handling the coach sides.

The use of 'Ellemsee' as a brand name after the war somewhat improved the consistency of labelling. Printed paper labels were used in some cases, in others printing, usually in blue, was direct onto the boxes. Boxes supplied from the late 1940s identified the LMC clearly whilst also carrying the Ellemsee name. From the mid 1950s onwards only the Ellemsee name was used, as on the box of chairs illustrated below right.

Appendix U   RAW MATERIALS AND TOOLS

The first modest offerings of raw materials from the Leeds Model Company, of pitch pine timber sections, followed the move to Harewood Street in 1921. Less than twelve months later the company, by then operating out of Balm Road Mills, was able to offer a wide range of steel and brass sections and flats, tinplate, wire, rivets and pins. In fact, something of every item used in their own manufacturing processes was available to buy.

There was every incentive in those early days to encourage enthusiasts to build from their own ideas and so develop their layouts. The range of tools offered by the company in support of this was extensive including pliers, hammers, screwdrivers, callipers, punches, hacksaw frames and blades, drill bits and hand drills, taps and tap wrenches, dies and die holders and Swiss files.

Stedman did not feature tools in his catalogue of 1929, but the 1927 range was replicated in the 1932 'Leeds Models Continued' listing, but not thereafter. Not that is until 1957, when the Agrippa screwdriver was promoted by the Company inside the front cover* of the modestly sized printed list.

Varying ranges of raw materials, including screws, nuts, bolts and washers were offered throughout the life of the company and remained to be sold off after liquidation.

Paints were also offered from 1922 until 1933, in the range of pre-grouping locomotive colours, plus white, red, red oxide, dark and light grey, and clear varnish. The colours dried to a semi-gloss finish, described as 'eggshell'. The advice, presumably reflecting painting practice in the factory was to finish the model with a coat of the special 'Engine Varnish' described as having *'great transparency'* **

*Incorrectly spelt as Agripra in the 1957 catalogue!

**Many fine paints are available today for both brushing and spraying to effect restorations, up to a full repaint. Satin finish auto sprays are particularly useful for black locomotives.

Appendix V   STEDMAN LINDON & CO LTD*

Adrian Stedman was involved with the affairs of S & B Productions even before his father's death. In 1958 he built, for S & B, two gravity die casting machines to use rubber multi-cavity dies, based on the successful methods long used by the LMC.

His company, Stedman Lindon & Co Ltd, had an office at 97 Broad Lane, Coventry and works at 25 Bull Head Lane Northampton. The company was advertised as 'Model Makers and Precision Engineers', but there are no details of other products or ventures in the Trust archives. His business partner was Bernard Lindon.

Early in 1969, Adrian met with Geoff Brown, who was already casting loco driving wheels for members of the Gauge '0' Guild. Brown expressed considerable interest in both the machines and the moulding materials, to add to and to improve his own product range.

Adrian was basing his proposals on a mould made from the then recently introduced silicone rubber which promised to provide both longer mould life and higher definition of casting details. Encouragement for the venture came from Leslie Scarlett who also strongly promoted the Guild, *'which has done a wonderful job over the last few years to bring together '0' gauge enthusiasts, and to act as a link with the trade'. He insisted that 'there was every likelihood of a resurgence in 7mm/ft, as witness at least two Continental manufacturers, Rivarossi and Pola-Maxi expanding production in this scale!'* Prophetic words indeed.

Ten years later Brown's production of wheels was still in full swing, but Stedman and Lindon's partnership did not last, Adrian's private practice, working on his own at home and widely abroad as a consulting plant engineer taking precedence.

*Brief details of this company serve to answer questions as to its relation to R.F. Stedman and the LMC.

INDEX OF DVD PICTURES

The model archive of the Leeds Stedman Trust

Picture No	Details of model	Year of manufacture
1	Series I standard 4-4-0T, SR 2664	1928
2	Series I standard 4-4-2T, LNER 6510	1925
3	Series I standard 0-4-4T, LMS 1213 ***	1926
4	Series I standard 0-6-2T, LNER 456	1929
5	0-4-0ST inside cylinder LNER 78	1937
6	0-4-0ST outside cylinder BR 68113	1952
7	GW 4-4-0 No 3837 'County of Stafford'**	1922
8	Caledonian 4-4-0 No 77 *	1922
9	GWR 2-6-0 'Mogul' No 4374 **	1928
10	LMS Ex Caledonian Pickersgill 0-6-0 No 17608	1929
11	LNER 4-4-0 Director No 5506 'Butler Henderson' *	1925
12	LNER 4-6-0 No 5427 'City of London' *	1926
13	LNER 4-6-0 No 1165 'Valour' **	1927
14	LNER Atlantic 4-4-2 No 1443 *	1923
15	GWR Star Class 4-6-0 No 4004 'Morning Star' **	1924
16	GWR Castle Class 4-6-0 No 4073 'Caerphilly Castle' **	1932
17	Midland Railway passenger coach No 578	1921
18	Midland Railway passenger full brake coach No 159	1921
19	North Eastern passenger coach No 840	1921
20	North Eastern passenger full brake coach No 106	1921
21	LNWR passenger coach No 2307	1921
22	LNWR passenger full brake coach No 5410	1921
23	MR passenger coach No 578 overprinted LMS	1925
24	MR passenger brake coach No 159 overprinted LMS	1925
25	LMS Brake composite coach No 358	1927
26	LNER twin articulated coaches Nos. 6021N and 6023N	1924
27	SR suburban coach No 4526	1927
28	SR suburban brake coach No 2127	1927
29	SR corridor coach No 4526	1927
30	SR corridor brake coach No 2127	1927
31	GWR panelled suburban coach No 3275	1927
32	GWR panelled suburban brake coach No 6927	1927
33	GWR panelled corridor coach No 3275	1927
34	GWR panelled corridor brake coach No 6927	1927

Note items 7 and 8 above are the locomotives made by LMC for Bassett-Lowke

Note: Acknowledgement is given for the professional repainting of locomotives by: * Alan Brackenborough, ** Ian Woodruff, *** Bob Stanley.

Other locomotives have been restored and repainted by David Peacock, or are as received, a few with original paintwork. All locomotives are in running order, but most do not have original mechanisms. All stock is in running order.

GLOSSARY

Bakelite
Bakelite was formulated by Belgian scientist Leo Baekeland between 1907 and 1909. It is a thermo-setting phenol formaldehyde resin usually filled with wood flour and coloured with various pigments. Bakelite is electrically non-conductive and has moderate heat resistance and stability. In 1993, Bakelite was designated a National Historical Chemical Landmark by the American Chemical Society in recognition of its significance as the world's first synthetic plastic.

Economiser
Economisers are (normally) large tube in shell heat exchangers for waste heat recovery on ships and land based power generation systems. Exact scale models would not only enable manufacturers such as Greens of Wakefield (who produced their first economiser in 1845) to demonstrate their products, but also assist through modelling with plant design and layout in situations where space was limited.

Gutland Railway
Gutland, the creation of Capt. William Kelly was started in the mid 1930s. The concept was an island in the English Channel where trains from the Continent and from the UK met and exchanged passengers, freight and motive power. Locomotives and rolling stock of both UK and French outline were among the original models, including several from LMC, running on the line. By repute the name Gutland was given to the railway by G.P. Keen, comparing the complexity of the layout to animal intestines. The name 'Anatomopolis' for the main station followed logically from this. On his death in 1961 Kelly left his railway to Keen, who in turn passed it across the Channel to Henri Girod-Eymery and his Museon de Rodo in Uzes. In 1980 Adrian Stedman was among the group of members of the Gauge '0' Guild visiting the museum. He took with him 4-4-0 Mansted Foundry 119 to run on the famous layout.

Injection Moulding
A method of component manufacture in which liquid plastic or molten metal is introduced to a mould cavity under pressure. See also pressure die casting.

Intergranular corrosion
A form of corrosion in which attack takes place preferentially at, and is concentrated on, the grain boundaries. This type of corrosion leads to swelling, cracking and disintegration before the bulk of the metallic mass has been

attacked to any considerable extent. Specific attack at the grain boundaries is due to the presence of impurities which accumulate there from detritus in the molten metal or segregate there as lower melting point alloys.

Pressure die casting
A process for making castings in which molten metal is forced into the mould or die under high pressure. The purpose is to obtain sound castings of high dimensional accuracy and good surface finish at a high rate of production.

Wakefield Cup
Lord Wakefield of Hythe sincerely believed that the world would benefit from an interest in aviation through the development of aero models. The rules of the competition for the Wakefield Cup determined that models must take off under their own power. Flight distance and duration would determine the winner. Any form of power could be used subject to a maximum model weight of 11 lbs (5 kgs). The first contest for the Wakefield Cup was held at Crystal palace in 1911 and won by Ernest Twining. Rex Stedman won the cup in the following year.

White metal
The generic name for a wide range of low melting point alloys of tin with copper, antimony, lead, zinc, iron and bismuth. Not all formulations contain all of the possible alloying elements, which vary according to required properties and end use. Hardness, strength and limited contraction on solidification, key considerations for model castings, dictate the formulation of alloys used. Other alloys, sometimes called 'white metal' which may be used include pewter, bearing (Babbitt) metals and fusible alloys which are predominantly tin based, and type metal in which the major constituent is lead.

SUBJECT INDEX

Models Railways and Locomotives (Magazine) 7, 12, 85
Model Railway News 15, 20, 22, 32, 38, 43, 48, 56, 57, 58, 59, 62, 67, 71, 72, 78, 103
Moore R.S. 8, 35, 45, 60, 103
Museon de Rodo (Uzes) 38,

National Railway Museum 38,
'Nettle' see Sentinel Railcar
'Newalloy' 5, 15, 43, 44, 48, 50, 53, 58, 81, 82, 83, 84, 86, 98, 100
'NON-LOK' buffers 44, 53, 61, 74,
North Eastern Railway
       Coaches *19, 20*, 24, **24**
       Locomotives, 8, **14**, **20**, **111**
              City of Ripon (Raven Pacific) 31, **31**
       Brake van and Wagons 13, **23**, 26, **26**, 28, *47*, *63*
Norwood Junction Models 11

Oil Tank Wagon 29, **30**, *76*

Patents (LMC/Stedman)
       Lithographs 13
       Smoke Units (provisional) 99
       Sprung axle guards (S&B) 11,
Palmer, Bruce 68,
Pantry Dockyard Railway 17, 39
Peacock, David (author) 4, 5 ,6, 73, 119, **Back Cover**
Peacock, Marcus 4, **76**
Potterdale Mills, Leeds 9, 48, 60, 69,
Potter, John B. 49, 70, 71, 72, 83,
Power supplies 108
Private Owner Wagons 27, **27**, 28, **30**, 45, *59-62*

Rathbone R. 60, 63, 69, 70, 71, 103
Raw Materials 115
REMOD wheels (Bing) 43,
R.F. Stedman & Co Ltd 4, 8, 29, 33, 34, 35, 36, 45, 47, 102, 105
Rigid litho coach 26, 61, *100*
Rolling Stock   Type A 23 - 28, **23**, **24**
               Type B 23, *64,66, 69-76*, **91-93**
               Type C 30, **30**
Royal Aircraft Factory (Farnborough) 7, 13, 31
Rush, Frederick 33, 35, 83, 103

S & B Productions 10, 11, 116
Scherzer bridges 31, **56**, 106
Sentinel railcar 'Nettle' 5, 28, 47, *68*, 72, 83, 93, 98
Shenphone 108
Signals 5, 40, 41, 104 - 5, **104**, **105**, 109, 110, 114
Simpson George M. 8, 22, 35, 45, 48, 60, 103